The heart of
Christmas

The heart of Christmas

Chris Leonard

Daily readings and reflections from Advent to Epiphany

Published by
The Bible Reading Fellowship
First Floor, Elsfield Hall
15–17 Elsfield Way, Oxford OX2 8FG
ISBN 1 84101 136 3

First published 2001
1 3 5 7 9 10 8 6 4 2 0

Acknowledgments

Unless otherwise stated, scripture quotations are taken from The New Revised Standard
Version of the Bible, Anglicized Edition, copyright © 1989, 1995 by the Division of
Christian Education of the National Council of the Churches of Christ in the USA,
and are used by permission. All rights reserved.

Scripture quotations taken from the Holy Bible, New International Version, copyright ©
1973, 1978, 1984 by International Bible Society, are used by permission of Hodder &
Stoughton Limited. All rights reserved. 'NIV' is a registered trademark of International Bible
Society. UK trademark number 1448790.

Scriptures quoted from the Good News Bible published by The Bible Societies/HarperCollins
Publishers Ltd, UK © American Bible Society 1966, 1971, 1976, 1992,
used with permission.

Extracts from the Authorized Version of the Bible (The King James Bible), the rights in
which are vested in the Crown, are reproduced by permission of the Crown's patentee,
Cambridge University Press.

Extracts from *The Alternative Service Book 1980* are copyright © The Archbishops' Council
and are reproduced by permission.

A catalogue record for this book is available from the British Library

Printed and bound in Great Britain by
Omnia Books Limited, Glasgow

Contents

Introduction

Most of us are over-busy at Christmas in one way or another—and that brings its own special kinds of difficulties, hilarious or otherwise. One mother I know had been working non-stop preparing to entertain fifteen for Christmas lunch. She thought everything was ready until her fireman husband arrived home from a late work-shift on Christmas Eve. 'What's that terrible smell?' he demanded, following his nose to the Aga, on top of which a huge turkey had been thawing for too long. The heat had turned the dead bird into salmonella's paradise. All they could do was wrap it in several layers of plastic and bury it at the top of the garden. But what would they eat the next day?

A cheerful type and good in a crisis, the husband said, 'Don't worry, I'll try the Christmas helpline!' He proceeded to explain the problem to the woman at the other end of the phone.

'Is this causing you great worry?' she asked.

'Well, only in that we're going to look pretty silly with no meat on the table tomorrow,' he replied.

'Do you normally become anxious when this kind of thing happens?'

'How do you mean, normally? If it had happened before, I'd know what to do now!'

'Can I ask if you're on any form of medication, for example anti-depressants or...?'

'No! Look, I'm not anxious and I'm not depressed. I just want to find out where I can get a turkey this late in the day!'

'I see. You do realize that you are through to the Samaritans?'

Apparently they were the only ones left manning the Christmas helpline.

Once he'd stopped laughing he remembered a turkey farm a few miles away. Early the next morning, he bought some very fresh meat there and everyone had plenty to eat.

Don't we all love Christmas… and loathe it? From childhood wonder onwards, we've all known special moments over the Christmas holiday. Yet faced with the peculiar pressures of the extended festive season these days, I, for one, find I need all the spiritual help I can get! It does me good, when in a 'Poor me!' mood, to remember that we all struggle with—and celebrate—different things. For this book, I've sought comments from people in many different circumstances and walks of life. I'd like to take this opportunity of thanking all of them for their time and honesty. They've proved what I've always suspected: talk to 'ordinary' (plus one or two well-known) Christians about their experiences and you'll hear some fascinating, extraordinary, funny, sad and humbling things. And a picture will build up of the way God really does come to be 'with us' in the realities of our lives, not just in church or on 'holy' (or holi-) days. All the stories are true, though sometimes individuals have asked that I preserve anonymity by changing various names.

But before reading about other people, it's good to stop for a few moments each day and explore what God says about the ups and downs of each of our lives at this time of year—from that first, distinctly uncomfortable Christmas Day onwards! There are six themes; each one includes a Bible reading from the first verses of John's Gospel and ends with one of the Beatitudes. All Bible quotes (unless otherwise indicated) are from the New Revised Standard Version.

ONE

Expectation or exhaustion?

Introduction

Is Advent really a time of expectation... or exhaustion? 'The first,' we're meant to chorus. 'The second!' I moan sometimes, drowning in paper of both work and wrapping varieties, longing for carefree childhood days and wishing I had more time to prepare for the celebration of Jesus' coming. Certainly we may experience this season of the year differently at different times in our lives. Young mother Helen Hotchkiss writes:

A Christmas Eve tradition! Packing, loading the car, locking up, then out on the icy roads at last. We leave behind a house deserted, half-heartedly decorated, graced with a tree that no one will see tomorrow, and set off on our annual winter trip to one or the other set of parents.

But not this year. There's a new baby, making us a 'real family' of four. So, instead, we'll be singing carols round our very own tree, tucking David into his little bed and waking up to our first ever Christmas at home. A chance to unwrap a new dimension of family life, taking time together and with our wider church family to remember that other baby and the new life he brings.

Perhaps the real difference that we feel lies not so much in our circumstances but in whether we are 'hype-driven' or 'light-called'. If we're hype-driven, we'll end up exhausted, running on empty. The few characters in the nativity story who left everything to be with Jesus, by contrast, were light-called by God through star or angel. To all those who come at his invitation, swapping their burden for his, he promises not freneticism and an early heart attack, but life—his own life!

My life for yours, Lord!

1 December

The word that Isaiah son of Amoz saw concerning Judah and Jerusalem: In days to come the mountain of the Lord's house shall be established as the highest of the mountains, and shall be raised above the hills; all the nations shall stream to it. Many peoples shall come and say, 'Come, let us go up to the mountain of the Lord, to the house of the God of Jacob; that he may teach us his ways and that we may walk in his paths.' For out of Zion shall go forth instruction, and the word of the Lord from Jerusalem. He shall judge between the nations, and shall arbitrate for many peoples; they shall beat their swords into ploughshares, and their spears into pruning hooks; nation shall not lift up sword against nation, neither shall they learn war any more. O house of Jacob, come, let us walk in the light of the Lord!

ISAIAH 2:1–5

Advent is a time of great expectations, and this passage proclaims great expectations indeed! But Isaiah wrote seven centuries before Jesus' birth and for most of those centuries Israel didn't follow God. Threatened, then overwhelmed, by a succession of superpowers, experiencing defeat in war and the humiliations of exile and captivity —why would other nations beat a path to Jerusalem in order to live in peace and worship the Jewish God there? The Jews tired of waiting. During the last four hundred years before Christ's birth, even the prophets turned silent.

By the time the Messiah appeared in Bethlehem, only a few people —like the shepherds, Herod and the wise men—took any notice of the momentous event. This baby wasn't much for angel choirs to sing about—conceived out of wedlock, born to a poor couple from unfashionable, occupied Galilee. Not the one, surely, to bring peace on earth, goodwill to all people. How could Isaiah's prophecy be fulfilled in him?

Even today we don't see lions lying down with lambs, or many stockpiles of weapons turned into agricultural implements. God is honoured, worshipped and obeyed throughout our planet, but not by everyone. That's reserved for when Jesus next comes, creating a new heaven and a new earth where sin and suffering will be no more. So we too are waiting. Despite all the amazing things Jesus and the Holy Spirit have done—despite the fact that, down the ages, Christians have fought against slavery, child labour and other enemies of peace—we've yet to see Isaiah's expectations fully realized.

Has God given us dreams, as he did to Joseph, only for us to see them buried in something which feels like a pit or prison? Have we been praying 'in full assurance of faith' for people we love, only to see them wander further into dangerous territory? Do we long to see God's kingdom come in our own community, claiming it for him as we walk the streets, serving and loving there, seeking opportunities to speak of the way he can change lives? Do we tire when, despite all this effort, very little appears to happen, when our influence is ignored, our love misinterpreted and our prayers fall on apparently deaf ears?

Advent is a time of waiting, a waiting for his time, which is not always our time. Jesus' birth only began to set things in motion. So did his resurrection and ascension, though they left his victory in no doubt. But we know that his heart's desire is for peace, justice and righteousness—and who else has the words of eternal life? This Advent, let's go on a journey together, praying, trusting and working with him—for his kingdom will come!

Garth Hewitt promotes justice and peace through music and storytelling. He told me:

This afternoon I was with Riah Abu el-Assal, the Anglican Bishop of Jerusalem. All Christians are on a journey towards the values of the Prince of Peace, but when you talk with people like him you realize the complexities and the cost. He's a Palestinian from Nazareth; an Israeli citizen, concerned for justice for his own people, who have been treated as second-class. He tries to live out the values of Luke 4:18–19: bringing good news to the poor, setting the oppressed free and so on.

He's a key figure at this time in Jerusalem—a city seen as holy to three different faiths and as capital to both Palestinian and Jew. He tries to protest for peace for the Palestinians while forwarding the road to peace between Palestinian and Jew and also furthering relationships among those of different faiths. But it is far from easy. If you're working for the kingdom of God to come, you're open to misunderstanding: for example, some Christians wanted Archbishop Tutu to keep right out of politics. But peace and justice aren't anaemic or other-worldly: working them out on the ground is gritty. I tell the stories of people like the bishop so that Christians living in an easy environment can pray with understanding and, where people are suffering, campaign on their behalf, or at least write and let them know they are not forgotten.

Your kingdom come, Lord; your will be done on earth as it is in heaven.

2 December

In the beginning was the Word, and the Word was with God, and the Word was God. He was in the beginning with God. All things came into being through him, and without him not one thing came into being. What has come into being in him was life, and the life was the light of all people.
JOHN 1:1–4

November's normally the busiest shopping month. By the time we reach the start of Advent, work deadlines loom and many of us feel exhausted. Since August, displays of Christmas cakes and puddings, of cards and tinsel, have pushed everyday items into corners where even the shop's shelf-fillers don't know where to find them. Every year I try to ignore the hype that urges us all not to be, but to buy, but I always end up scurrying about, panicking that things won't be ready—as if it mattered. Somehow every year the pressure to create a 'perfect Christmas' gets to me and Stressville rules OK.

At the beginning of Advent, our thoughts turn to the one we expect to come. So who is he—this longed-for Jewish Messiah, this Saviour who changed a world order, this God who emptied himself and came to live among us, this King of kings who sets the great pivotal points of history, making ends and beginnings? John introduces him in a way that contrasts abruptly with our often frantic activity. He 'was'. At the beginning the Word wasn't actually speaking or doing anything. He simply... was, with God, the One whose name and nature is I AM, or I WILL BE WHAT I WILL BE. The only break in their relationship, the only thing to come between them, occurred during the brief hours when Jesus took our sin upon himself on the cross. And after that, he went and *sat down* at the right hand of God.

Out of that stillness and relationship, something quite astounding happened! 'All things came into being through him... what came into being in him was life and the life was the light of all people.' From his stillness came a great river of life—all this teeming, noisy world, full of action and change and colour and movement and variety. Day and night; breathing out and breathing in; jostling molecules and expanding galaxies; music, art and innovative ideas; tenderness and passion... life in all its fullness, never for one moment boring! Activity is not the enemy if it comes from Jesus, who upholds the universe by the word of his power.

Simply being with God—most of us are not there yet. Maybe we can look for, expect, make room for a little bit of simply being with him this Advent.

Being with someone (let alone God): what does that mean? Being with certain people: doesn't it make you feel better, even if you don't exchange a single word? Jane Cornford, a busy secretary and mother of two teenagers, writes:

Around Christmas-time last year, a long illness and family worries had left me feeling worn down. Then something distressed me immediately before we went to church. Struggling to fight back my tears there, I found myself sitting next to an old lady I'd never seen before. During my feeble attempt at being a 'friendly Christian', I learnt she was a retired missionary visiting her sister who happened to live in our village. The service started soon after, so we said very little but somehow her presence gave me strength and hope. She must have been through a great deal on the mission field in Zaire, and seen some terrible things. Now widowed and alone, she radiated only warmth, love, faith and well-being. If angels are messengers, then God sent an angel to sit next to me that day—and all she did was simply to be there, and be in love with him!

Lord, even though the night may be dark and stormy, and your light is shining far away, as though through the window of some distant house, help me to keep my eyes fixed on you during this

Advent time. Help me to avoid anything unnecessary which blocks my vision, any obstacles which would prevent me from walking towards you. Strengthen me to hold your word as a lamp for my feet, as I take each step nearer to you who are calling me.

3 December

When the men had come to him, they said, 'John the Baptist has sent us to you to ask, "Are you the one who is to come, or are we to wait for another?"' Jesus had just then cured many people of diseases, plagues, and evil spirits, and had given sight to many who were blind. And he answered them, 'Go and tell John what you have seen and heard: the blind receive their sight, the lame walk, the lepers are cleansed, the deaf hear, the dead are raised, the poor have good news brought to them. And blessed is anyone who takes no offence at me.'
LUKE 7:20–23

People had great expectations of John the Baptist. Before he was born the angel said to his father, Zechariah, 'You will have joy and gladness, and many will rejoice at his birth, for he will be great in the sight of the Lord… Even before his birth he will be filled with the Holy Spirit. He will turn many of the people of Israel to the Lord their God' (Luke 1:14–16). Wow! Someone yet to be conceived would do all this? More! 'With the spirit and power of Elijah he will go before him, to turn the hearts of parents to their children, and the disobedient to the wisdom of the righteous, to make ready a people prepared for the Lord' (1:17).

The waiting must have seemed an age to Zechariah, struck dumb for his unbelief from before the conception until the naming ceremony, eight days after the baby's birth. His voice restored, Zechariah prophesied, 'You, child, will be called the prophet of the Most High; for you will go before the Lord to prepare his ways, to give knowledge of salvation to his people by the forgiveness of their sins. By the tender mercy of our God, the dawn from on high will break upon us, to give light to those who sit in darkness and in the shadow of death, to guide our feet into the way of peace' (Luke 1:76–79).

More waiting: 'The child grew and became strong in spirit, and he was in the wilderness until the day he appeared publicly in Israel' (Luke 1:80). Did his elderly parents ever see that day? We don't know. Nor do we know why God trains so many of his agents in the wilderness—Abraham, Moses, Joshua, even Jesus. In the end, crowds flocked to the wild man of the desert, to hear his stark message of repentance, be submerged in the muddy river Jordan and wonder at his proclamation that 'one who is more powerful than I is coming' (Luke 3:16).

But if others had great expectations of him, John had far greater expectations of Jesus. However, such expectations didn't prevent John, or Jesus, being killed—and for what? A few people changed their lifestyle for a while, were healed, or brought closer to God until the events of Good Friday sounded the death knell of all hope, all expectation.

Then the resurrection and subsequent release of the promised Holy Spirit upon ordinary men and women changed everything. Jesus said, 'I tell you, among those born of women no one is greater than John; yet the least in the kingdom of God is greater than he.' If much was expected of John, who succeeded in preparing the way for Jesus, more is expected of us, for whom Jesus has prepared the way!

I asked some children what they expect of Jesus—at Christmas and generally—and what they think he expects of them.

I get truly excited about Christmas but when I open my presents (usually, anyway) I remember that this is the day when Jesus was born. I expect that he'll help me—not, you know, completely sort things out, but make things better. He does help me when I pray. I broke up with my best friend because her mum doesn't like me at all. Jesus does encourage me and makes me feel a bit better about it and I think he will help us to be friends again. I pray that every night.

I'm not sure what he expects of me. I think he expects me to get to know him better. I keep a Bible in the drawer next to my bed and I like reading the stories in it and finding out what God does.

DEBBIE, AGED 8

Christmas is Jesus' birthday, so you hear about him a lot—there are special things happening at school and at church, and all that makes me think about him more. I pray more. The rest of the year I do pray if something goes wrong but I don't expect an answer so much as I do at Christmas.

At Christmas I thank him for everything and I do expect to feel or hear him talking back. He does, I think, though I'm not always sure if it really is him or if it's me talking to myself. Sometimes I do hear his voice but mainly it's like thoughts inside my head—and that's when I'm not sure if it's me just imagining it, so I ask him and then usually I kind of feel him there. It's hard to describe.

School's hard because most of my friends don't believe in Jesus and I often hide that I do. I think he expects me not to hide that I believe in him and also to spend more time with him. He hasn't spoken to me about what he wants for my whole life like he did with John the Baptist. Sometimes I think he does ask me to do things, but usually I don't do them because I'm not sure if it really is him asking or if it's just me making it up.

ANNA, AGED 11

Emmanuel, you are 'God with us'—now, at Christmas, in the New Year and for eternity. Thank you that you don't get tired of waiting for us. This Christmas time I think about the expectations I have of you... What do you expect of me?

4 December

I will extol you, my God and King, and bless your name for ever and ever. Every day I will bless you, and praise your name for ever and ever. Great is the Lord and greatly to be praised; his greatness is unsearchable. One generation shall laud your works to another, and shall declare your mighty acts. On the glorious splendour of your majesty, and on your wondrous works, I will meditate. The might of your awesome deeds shall be proclaimed, and I will declare your greatness. They shall celebrate the fame of your abundant goodness, and shall sing aloud of your righteousness. The Lord is gracious and merciful, slow to anger and abounding in steadfast love. The Lord is good to all, and his compassion is over all that he has made. All your works shall give thanks to you, O Lord, and all your faithful shall bless you. They shall speak of the glory of your kingdom, and tell of your power, to make known to all people your mighty deeds, and the glorious splendour of your kingdom.

PSALM 145:1–12

During this Advent period there are plenty of opportunities to celebrate God's goodness as well as to 'eat, drink and be merry':

- Carol concerts and 'scratch' performances of Handel's *Messiah*.
- A pipe organ vibrating though a vast cathedral, resonating within our hearts and bodies.
- The lighting of the first candle at the start of Advent. Though small and vulnerable, it brings hope of spreading light to others and, eventually, the world!
- Nativity plays where, even today, five-year-olds do still praise God's works in front of their parents and grandparents, declaring his mighty acts in ways which melt the hardest of hearts.

- The greeting of one another at midnight on Christmas Eve. Made one through sharing his body and his blood, together we celebrate the first moments of his birthday.

If we're always waiting, waiting for Christmas Day itself, as the hype encourages us to do, we'll miss much along the way and feel let down if the day itself doesn't live up to its promise. In the midst of all the preparations and deadlines, even beneath the tattered tinsel and pagan mistletoe in the workplace, we can choose to meditate for a moment on the words of the great carols. They may be churned out by an annoying sleigh-mounted tape machine in the High Street: 'Hark, the herald angels sing "Glory!" to the newborn king. Peace on earth and mercy mild—God and sinners reconciled!' But such words come straight from the Bible and it is good to meditate on the glorious splendour of his majesty and on his wondrous works. Never mind our expectations, he's done so much already! Wonder still attaches itself to the Christmas period, eternity still draws near—which may be why even those who ignore Jesus for most of the year often come along to one or more Christmas services to join the celebrations of his birth.

So, do all his works give thanks to him? Walking across the church car park at half past midnight one Christmas morning, we heard a blackbird singing through the frosty air. A cynic would argue that the neon street-lights had kept him awake, so he'd decided to proclaim his territory, but as we listened to the clear beauty of his song we preferred to think that the blackbird, like us, was celebrating Jesus' birth.

Concert pianist David McArthur was invited to play on the QE2 and, along with his wife and two teenage children, embarked on a Caribbean Christmas Cruise from 14 December to 5 January. 'It must have been quite a celebration!' I said to him.

Well, yes! It was strange, though—very hot. We were strolling around on deck late at night, wearing shorts and sandals. And then, I suppose for most people Christmas means, above all, a family time. Perhaps some of the passengers didn't get on with their family or had none and were looking to celebrate with a ready-made social group. They weren't always the happiest of people. No one forced jollity on them, though. You could choose from a real mixture of activities—for example, on Christmas Day, anything from, would you believe, step aerobics to a skincare clinic; from a 'Snowball Bonanza Bingo' to an interdenominational service led by the ship's captain. I was playing that night, so there was no alcohol for me all day and no Christmas dinner either—I can't eat before I play! I did a total of four concerts on the cruise but demands on the piano meant that my slot for essential daily practice came before eight each morning. There's no point going to bed early on a cruise, so I ran up quite a sleep deficit.

I asked if he would rather celebrate Christmas at home, or on a cruise.

Difficult question! We all had a great time but it wasn't normal. We worried a bit that our teenagers would think it was—and expect similar every year! I missed our traditions—keeping in touch with the wider family by phone, going to church, all that. The 'traditional carol service', led by ship's staff used to calling bingo or cheerleading children, felt more like the blind leading the blind than a spiritual experience! The ocean and the sky—the vastness of it all—spoke far more to me of God.

I certainly didn't regret missing the whole commercial build-up. As a family, we decided that a cruise was enough and gave each other tiny presents. We avoided the last-minute rush to send cards and the annual scrummage around ridiculously crowded shops. So, on balance, I do prefer celebrating Christmas at home but a cruise comes a pretty close second and we were very fortunate to have experienced it!

> *Earth's crammed with heaven*
> *And every common bush afire with God;*
> *But only he who sees, takes off his shoes,*
> *The rest sit round it and pluck blackberries.*
> FROM 'AURORA LEIGH' BY ELIZABETH BARRETT BROWNING (1806–61)

Wherever we are, Lord—at home, in the office, on the train, on holiday—help us to see you, to take off our shoes and worship.

5 December

The Lord is faithful in all his words, and gracious in all his deeds. The Lord upholds all who are falling, and raises up all who are bowed down. The eyes of all look to you, and you give them their food in due season. You open your hand, satisfying the desire of every living thing. The Lord is just in all his ways, and kind in all his doings. The Lord is near to all who call to him, to all who call to him in truth. He fulfils the desire of all who fear him; he also hears their cry, and saves them. The Lord watches over all who love him, but all the wicked he will destroy. My mouth will speak the praise of the Lord, and all flesh will bless his holy name for ever and ever.

PSALM 145:13–21

Someone whose life had been a mess but who had newly discovered God's kindness might be able to say these words in perfect truth. But are they always true? Christians do fall. Some believers looking to him in a famine situations do die of hunger. His kindness is not always apparent, nor do we always feel him near. We expect so much of him and often receive it, but not always, as other psalms show. Psalm 88 is the most extreme example. Far from raising the psalmist up, God himself has put him 'in the depths of the Pit' and 'caused my companions to shun me… every day I call on you, O Lord… why do you hide your face from me… I suffer your terrors, I am desperate.' The situation is not resolved. The psalm ends, 'You have taken my companions and loved ones from me; the darkness is my closest friend' (NIV).

Advent, a time of expectation in both the secular and Christian sense, can be desperately hard for some people. But the real Christmas story isn't at all cosy. Even as a baby, Jesus suffered. God's promised rewards are to those who share in his sufferings, not to those who live a charmed life. His promises *are* true, but they have gritty depths—and it's important we stay real in our expectations.

For carers in particular, Christmas can prove a demanding time. By 1998, Rosemary White's dad had been living with her family for nearly nine years and she and her husband had boys of 12 and 9 to consider. She writes:

Dad had reached his 90s. He was good-natured and hated to be any trouble, but because of his age he sometimes did potentially dangerous things, so we didn't like to leave him too much. It became harder to balance the demands of caring for him with those of our family and of the church.

As we approached Christmas, a nasty virus struck. My younger son was in hospital overnight and the next day my husband and other son succumbed. Soon Dad caught it too and was even more seriously affected because of his age. I alone kept well and struggled to look after my four men, but I had to cancel everything else. It had become a bit of a tradition in the Christmas morning service for my husband to play the organ and I the keyboard. My husband was just well enough to play, but I had to find a substitute because Dad was too ill to leave.

Eventually the virus subsided and Dad enjoyed another three years with us, but long-term caring for an elderly person with deteriorating faculties wore me down slowly. I often felt guilty that I was not kinder and more loving. Although I had always been very fond of my father, it was hard not to be impatient with him. At times he didn't seem like the same person.

When I felt I could not carry on much longer, I cried to the Lord for help. I dreaded the thought of telling Dad that I couldn't look after him any more. I am so thankful that I never had to do that, for not long after, Dad died peacefully after just a week's illness in hospital.

Lord, thank you for all the good things that you give—the beauty of the world around us, the riches we find in the companionship of others, for music, food and laughter, giving and receiving, creativity and variety, for your love, joy and peace. And when we endure times when we have none of those things, help us to love you for who you are, trusting that your great hand will cradle us through.

6 December

'Blessed are the poor in spirit, for theirs is the kingdom of heaven.'
MATTHEW 5:3

The Introduction to these first six reflections asked the question, 'Are we hype-driven or light-called?' In this age of instant everything, it can seem as though we keep chasing our ever-increasing expectations up spiral staircases which encircle emptiness and lead nowhere. While children in days gone by might have been content to hoot with laughter as Granny let her hair down acting in a family game of charades, now they sulk until they've gained sole possession of their latest PlayStation shooting extravaganza. But it's not only some children who end up dissatisfied through expecting life to be one long theme park ride, minus the queues. Our Christmas decorations have become 'unfashionable'. The jumbo freezer we'd need to store all the food we're urged to buy ready for the festive period simply wouldn't fit in our house! Constant expectation of more thrills, clothes, sexual excitement, faster cars, more money, better holidays, bigger houses and ever more spectacular worship and preaching leave us discontented and exhausted in our efforts to obtain them. Drivenness, stress, nervous exhaustion, workaholism, addiction, keeping up with the Joneses—all of these are typical of an age in which we have more and more, yet less and less in terms of things that really matter, like peace of mind and lasting good relationships.

On the other hand, those who are light-called know that they are in darkness. They know that they are poor and it doesn't worry them, because, as Jesus said, 'Life is more than food, and the body more than clothing.' He continued, 'Strive for his kingdom, and these things will be given to you as well' (Luke 12:23, 31).

So ours is the kingdom of heaven… if we are poor. If we're not, Jesus said, 'Sell your possessions, and give alms. Make purses for yourselves that do not wear out, an unfailing treasure in heaven, where no thief comes near and no moth destroys. For where your treasure is, there your heart will be also' (Luke 12:33–34). Hard words to an affluent society. Most of us haven't sold all our goods and given them to the poor. It's too risky to trust God that much, to admit that we are poor in spirit and cannot rely on our own efforts. Perhaps that explains why we are more often hype-driven than light-called— working to eat and eating to work, with a bit of sleep and leisure and worship thrown in and very little time to care for the poor, care for each other or care for God. Yet the poor shepherds left their flocks in the field and the wise men their rich environment, to be with Jesus.

Too radical, too impractical? Probably. How do we get from here to there? I don't know, but I suspect it involves that uncomfortable word, obedience—and the giving not only of money but of time. Let's pray that, this Advent, all of us may follow the light more than the hype. May it be a time not of great but of right expectations, expectations of his kingdom—his rule and reign—being outworked in our lives and our communities.

Liz Babbs, a teacher and dancer, was healed of ME nine years ago and has helped many others through her book *Can God Help M.E.?* Knowing what it is to lose her health and mobility and all that goes with them, she writes:

With the success of my book and an influx of invitations to speak, dance, write, lead retreats etc, as well as teach, I'm having to learn how to say 'no'.

Last year, saying 'no' was not a problem; in fact I longed to say 'yes'! After a year and a half of disability—the result of a serious knee injury—I began to walk unaided for the first time. And so Christmas last year was special—special because I discovered the gift of walking. Even the experience of going Christmas shopping thrilled me because I was seeing things through new eyes. I had become like a child again—excited by the lights and colours and smells. The sheer sparkle of it all dazzled me. How could I have taken all this for granted before? And why is it that it is only when something is taken away from me that I begin to value it and to realize the treasures that lie in ordinary everyday life?

The challenge this year is to remember—remember all that God has so generously given to me and to be thankful for the rich tapestry of friendships that he has woven together in my life.

Restore to us, dear Lord, the joy of your salvation. Help us to lay aside our self-sufficiency and simply wonder. Help us to understand that it is not within our power to rush around putting everything right in our world, but to respond like loved and obedient children when you ask us to put our piece of your jigsaw in place.

TWO

Joy or disappointment?

Introduction

One last check through the boot of the car. Yes, they had all the presents! It would be good spending Christmas with mum-in-law, Fiona thought as Steve drove them up the motorway. But when they arrived, a miserable mum-in-law said her boyfriend (if someone in his 50s could be called a 'boyfriend') had left, taking half the furniture in the flat. He'd even taken the mattress from the double bed in the spare room.

By next morning Fiona and Steve had concluded that sleeping on a bed-base wasn't realistic. No one felt exactly cheerful while opening their presents on Christmas Day—and to make matters worse, the dog chose that precise moment to keel over with a heart attack. I've had enough, thought Fiona—and locked herself in the bathroom for three hours, fuming. She'd been slaving away teaching all term and now... 'Without the trimmings, Lord, what on earth is Christmas all about?' she asked.

Christmas can certainly bring out the best and the worst in people. It can result in acute disappointment or be a time for joy, wonder and true celebration.

7 December

The light shines in the darkness, and the darkness did not overcome it.
JOHN 1:5

However much it once glowed gold against a blue sky, finally the northern hemisphere's October slides into dank November. Crisp leaves turn to slush underfoot. By now, in early December, the working day both starts and ends in darkness, enlivened by the garish lights on Santa's plastic sleigh. TV screens pulse with allurements, blatant or bizarre, to buy yet more toys or perfume. Christmas lights that shine in the darkness are not like they used to be, we think, nor what they're meant to be. What a let-down!

But Christmas doesn't mean pretending that everyone basks cosily in the best of all possible worlds. Jesus was born into a dark and hostile environment—his country under occupation, his hard-pressed parents far from home, his 'cosy manger' prickly, cold and unhygienic. It seems fitting that some of us celebrate the dawning of his light at the darkest time of our year.

Many find real joy in the Christmas season, and look forward all year to the gatherings of family and friends, to the Christmas plays and carols, to giving presents with love and to a special time celebrating the birth of Jesus. And that's great. But for a number, family tensions, unfulfilled expectations or loss make it a time of added pain and stress.

So today let's remember the biblical truth that, however stressed or disillusioned we may feel, however dark our circumstances, darkness does not overcome (seize, possess, grab hold of) the light. Indeed, in a dark room a candle will appear far brighter than in a sunny one. The festive season throbs with artificial lights—from Rudolf, with his 'very shiny nose', to the perfect families in ads, their faces aglow courtesy of the gas company. All these may hide the true light but they cannot put it out.

That light, which flickered into this world in the shape of a vulnerable baby, not only survived to manhood, but lives still, through his Holy Spirit, in the hearts of millions of people all over this planet. Far more than Marilyn Monroe or Princess Diana, Jesus lived his life on earth like a candle blowing in the wind. Like them, he died young, yet unlike them he lives today, still kindling hope and compassion, still sparking desire to liberate the oppressed, still empowering the weak and meek, making blind people see, bringing them joy as he lights their path to God.

Mother-of-three Joy Piper is a Christian who suffers from Seasonally Affective Disorder. She writes:

It's that time of year again. The hours of daylight are rapidly shrinking, the sun only gives a feeble, watery light on the days when it condescends to grace us with its presence, and we're heading far too rapidly into the dark, cold days of winter. It's not the favourite season of most people, but for the small percentage of the population who suffer from more than mere winter blues, it's a case of 'grit the teeth hard, get as much light as you can, and remember spring will come again one day'—hopefully.

SAD sufferers need good-quality light if the chemicals responsible for passing messages around their brains are to work properly—which is why you'll find me tucked up in the study with my breakfast tray and the TV news programmes, every morning from September to April, in front of a small wooden box about the size of a stereo speaker. This device emits a powerful light, equivalent to a bright summer dawn, or 10,000 candle-power. (For comparison, the brightest ordinary light bulb or fluorescent tube is under 500). After two hours of that shining on to me, I'm ready for the day. Without it, I become morose and sink into hibernation. Not very appropriate for someone called Joy!

For me, as a Christian, the treatment I have to undergo for so much of the year has brought a whole new depth of meaning to the imagery of light in the Bible. The change which the light-box has brought about in me is nothing short of miraculous—as has been the change in me since I first let Jesus, the Light of the world, become my boss, my 'Lord', nearly 32 years ago. The light-box has become a symbol—a constant reminder to me that, just as I must gaze at it each morning in order to generate the physical resources to cope with the day ahead, so it is wise to spend time at the opening of every day in quiet contemplation of Jesus, my spiritual light. Then, and only then, can I live each day to its fullest potential, with him and for him.

Without light... without him... I soon come a cropper, at any time of the year. How about you?

It will be Christmas soon. We'll be surrounded by candles and twinkling fairy lights. Let's pray that our eyes will be focused on the true Light whose coming into the world we celebrate at this season. And let's remember with compassion all those who are sad, who cannot join in with the joy and laughter for whatever reason, and prayerfully entrust them into his loving, healing care.

Maybe you could light a candle and, as you sit quietly and look at it, ask God to speak to you about his light shining in the darkness. What is he saying to you?

Lighten our darkness, Lord, we pray; and in your mercy, defend us from all perils and dangers of this night; for the love of your only Son, our Saviour, Jesus Christ.

COLLECT FOR EVENING PRAYER (ASB)

8 December

I was envious of the arrogant; I saw the prosperity of the wicked. For they have no pain; their bodies are sound and sleek. They are not in trouble as others are; they are not plagued like other people. Therefore pride is their necklace; violence covers them like a garment. Their eyes swell out with fatness; their hearts overflow with follies. They scoff and speak with malice; loftily they threaten oppression. They set their mouths against heaven, and their tongues range over the earth. Therefore the people turn and praise them, and find no fault in them.

PSALM 73:3–10

The psalmist is disappointed, angry and not a little envious of those who get rich by hurting others. I guess most of us react in the same way sometimes, though we might not be honest enough to speak to God about it.

Christmas can bring out the best or the worst in people: Christmas spirits of the alcoholic variety often lead to obscenities or violence. Globally, too, things haven't changed much since the psalmist's day, despite the coming of Jesus. Each Advent, the news brings stories of wars and brutality. Tyrants still oppress. Terrorists choose Christmas time to perpetrate atrocities: remember Lockerbie or IRA bombing campaigns in London? Nothing disappoints and angers like injustice —when we see the kindest people racked with terrible pain, physical or emotional, whereas those who couldn't care less, who trample over others on their way to the top, grow sound and sleek, self-satisfied and 'fat'.

We may start questioning. What does God think he is doing? Doesn't he care about justice? Has he turned his back on us or become impotent? If God minded us asking these questions, the Bible wouldn't contain verses such as these. If we listen patiently, we may hear God's heartbeat, his point of view.

Dave Hodson serves as a police officer with the Met in central London. I know he must see more 'wickedness' than most, yet he never appears hard or cynical. What does he make of the downside of human behaviour over the Christmas period?

People try to drive back from staff parties when they're too drunk to walk or speak and some end up crashing their cars, losing their jobs and wrecking their lives, to say nothing of other people's. It makes me sad. So does finding out why homeless people are sleeping on the streets. One young chap told me he'd never go back home because his father abused him. Others are mentally ill but don't cause trouble and so they remain forgotten. When the 'Crisis' shelter closes after Christmas, it's often the coldest time of year. Some of the charities are doing a great job, yet so many vagrants need ongoing practical help. I'd like to see more being done.

Yes, people who live outside city centres haven't a clue as to what goes on—and not only among the poor. We were called to a collapse—a man in his mid-30s, living alone in a flat worth half a million. We found him unconscious and naked on his bedroom floor, amid the most fantastic furniture and piles of human excrement. He'd picked up a transvestite prostitute in Kings Cross, asked 'her' to get him drugs and inject them in his arm with her own needle. After having sex he'd collapsed with an overdose. Was it a cry for help that made him dice with death like that? It's hard to understand people's behaviour.

Another time we picked up a shoplifter from Harvey Nics—a heroin addict with AIDS. Her two pimps made her steal to order before they'd supply her with drugs—and clients. She lived with her two small kids in the same tiny council flat where she entertained those clients. I felt dreadfully sad, and angry at the whole vicious spiral. How could men be that callous towards women and children?

I used to be cynical but becoming a Christian a few years ago helped me find more compassion. Shortly after that, we were called to a fight. A large drunk had just punched his pregnant girlfriend in the stomach, broken a female police officer's nose and floored her male colleague. He kept swearing and threatening the six officers restraining him, making unwholesome suggestions about our wives and mothers. I felt an overwhelming compassion for him. My colleagues couldn't understand why I was praying for him, after all he'd done. I replied with something along the lines that he needed help and this was the only way he was going to get it, through God's intervention in his life.

In most cases I'll never know the results of my prayers. But one time a huge female mental patient had walked out of her ward and locked herself in her daughter's flat. The previous time it happened, out of ten policemen restraining her, two got injured. She was ranting and raving from a first-floor window, threatening to pour boiling water over us. While some of the younger PCs were putting on defensive gear, I attempted to calm her down. It was only when she kept quoting from the Bible, interspersed with terrible cursing and sexual language, that I thought of praying. I looked her in the eye and prayed that somehow God's love would reach her. Quietly she disappeared back into the flat. I prayed that God would send someone who could resolve the situation. As a former colleague of mine walked round the corner, the woman emerged, said, 'I'll speak with that man' and came down the stairs like a lamb. As she got in the ambulance she pointed at me and said, 'I hate you!'

Another time, at a Worthington Cup Final at Wembley, we'd been briefed to expect trouble and hardcore hooligans. Sure enough, before the match, fights kept starting, inside the ground and out. Amid the chaos we made numerous arrests. Only when the match started did I have time to pray for God's peace to come, and it was really strange. I saw a hand hovering over the stadium. After the match, when the worst trouble had been expected, there wasn't a single incident or arrest—not even any chanting. My sergeant said, 'I don't understand this!' I didn't dare tell him about God answering prayer!

Pray for all those whose experiences of the dark side of life have robbed them of their joy and trust in God—and thank God that he does get involved and answers prayer.

9 December

Whom have I in heaven but you? And there is nothing on earth that I desire other than you. My flesh and my heart may fail, but God is the strength of my heart and my portion for ever. Indeed, those who are far from you will perish; you put an end to those who are false to you. But for me it is good to be near God; I have made the Lord God my refuge, to tell of all your works.

PSALM 73:25–28

'There is nothing on earth that I desire other than you.' Taken alone, that sounds impossibly austere. But the words don't spell gloom: 'I'll give up everything to be a deprived Christian for the rest of my life!' No, this sublime love song is like that moment of solemn joy when marriage partners, passionate for one another, promise to love for better, for worse; for richer, for poorer; in sickness or in health—until death parts them. Only, in this case, death will only improve the relationship, which really can last for ever!

We make life so complicated with our conflicting desires—setting ourselves up for disappointment. At Christmas we have to have the right food, the right presents and the right decorations. We have to go with the right people to the right parties. And, if anything upsets our carefully laid plans—if people are ill at the last minute… if they don't like our cooking or the expensive panto… if the children sulk and squabble or Aunt Sophie causes trouble again, despite all our efforts—we're so disappointed.

If we desired nothing but God, we would save ourselves a lot of strife, but is that realistic? Some religions encourage people to forget all about the world around them and lose themselves in religious devotion. Our God commands something far more difficult—to love our neighbour as ourselves. And that's where many of us struggle. In trying to love people, we are bound to encounter frustration and disappointment, especially during the Christmas season when everything is supposed to be perfect, but in practice never is.

If we were in heaven, sin, selfishness and suffering would be unknown and everyone would love and give and worship the Lamb with a pure heart. But on earth the joy which is our strength is going to be tempered with disappointment that things are not as God intended.

In the end, God will sort things out. That which is false will perish. He will create a new heaven and a new earth. In the meantime, Advent lasts for more than the few weeks preceding each Christmas. In this spoilt but still beautiful world, we wait for his second Advent. Before the fulfilment of his plans we have simple (though not easy) instructions: to nestle close to him, making him our refuge; to 'tell of all his works'; and to do what Jesus would do. As we share in the fellowship of his suffering—and disappointments—we are promised the far greater joy of his resurrection and of his presence with us.

Shirley Chapman spent over thirty years with one other missionary in a remote, roadless part of Brazil, translating the Bible for the Paumarí tribe and acting as their midwife and medical adviser. She writes:

From childhood I had grown up with the familiar sights of Christmas around me—bright lights and decorations, special food and family gatherings, nativity scenes, decorated trees and presents. How different to find myself in the Amazon rain-forest—hot and humid in a very wet rainy season; no shops; no electricity, let alone fancy lights; no special food. Trees grew everywhere, but none was decorated with bulging mounds of presents beneath. The one genuine similarity between both kinds of Christmas was... Jesus.

As we told the Paumarí the story of Christ's birth and the whole gospel, slowly a church was born. Some years later, in front of a packed audience who had never experienced a play before, new believers acted out the nativity scene. No substitute doll here, but a mother and her few-days-old baby! The Christmas story unfolded as they read newly translated passages from a language which had not been written down until we arrived.

'Whom have I in heaven but you?' It felt strange those first years to be celebrating Christmas so far from home, and yet we were declaring the same truth—'God with us'. Yes, he was indeed our 'strength' and our 'refuge' but it is good also 'to tell of all his works'. In addition, the Paumarí had become my family and I part of their kinship system, a second mother to the babies I'd delivered. Love came down at Christmas not just for our Western nations, but for the remote, forgotten peoples of this world—to be a light shining in their darkness and poverty.

Jesus, thank you for giving me the privilege of seeing you come to the Paumarí people. Please send your children who have heard the story so many times to take it to the two thousand other people groups who still await it in darkness.

May the genuineness of our faith, being more precious than gold, result in praise and glory when Jesus Christ is revealed.

ADAPTED FROM 1 PETER 1:8

10 December

The kingdom of God is not food and drink but righteousness and peace and joy in the Holy Spirit.
ROMANS 14:17

I laughed out loud at an e-mail that a friend sent me in late November. It concluded, 'Must go, as have to clean out tarantulas, redecorate house, inject Christmas pudding with triple vodkas and prepare scintillating column for *Perfect Christian Woman* magazine.' Yes, and construct a donkey costume for little Clothilda's school play, be in seven places at once to satisfy the demands of the family's pre-Christmas diary and somehow divine what various male in-laws want for Christmas... Sorry, but there's no time for righteousness, peace and joy in the Holy Spirit as well. What a shame!

'How was your Christmas?' I overheard one shop assistant say to another on 27 December, their first day back at work.

'OK, I s'pose,' she replied.

'Really? Everyone else says, "What's the point?" You eat too much, you drink too much and you sit in front of the stupid telly!'

Today's verse is God's way of saying, 'Get a life!' He's not anti-food or drink or celebrations. You could say he invented them all. Jesus said, 'The thief comes only to steal and kill and destroy. I came that they may have life, and have it abundantly' (John 10:10). Despite his limited years and possessions, he had such a full life. He loved to feast but could fast too. He valued time with an individual (Mary or the woman at the well) more than food and its preparation. He could communicate on a deep level with anyone—rich or poor, old or young, male or female, respectable or despised—unless they had already hardened their hearts. Ordinary people loved to be with him and he told the most wonderful stories, speaking pithy wisdom in such a way that everyone knew it to be true. He feared no one, arguing like the most skilful barrister with priests, dictators and the devil himself. He multiplied picnics, enlivened weddings, wrecked funerals, silenced thunder and walked on water. In fact, he had so much life that death could not hold him—because he knew righteousness, peace and joy in the Holy Spirit. And we are called to follow him, whatever the season.

Mike Stanbrook, Risk Control Adviser for an international chocolate-making company, writes:

OK, so friends and family think I have the ideal job. According to my children, Ben and Julia, 'Dad goes around the world tasting chocolate.' Yes, I do travel internationally and, yes, I do work for the company bearing 'the first name in chocolate' but my job is a lot more involved than simply eating our products straight off the line. For a start, I need to ensure that our factories are safe places to work, that they won't catch fire and that our products will reach the shop shelves in good condition. Then I need to discuss business issues with management and, sometimes, lead seminars with key personnel. It's always a busy job and just because it's Christmas there is no relaxation!

To be honest, looking at the products we make in some factories, you'd think we'd confused the seasons—we make Christmas novelties in July, Valentine's Day boxes in November and Easter eggs in December. But preparation is all part of working in a fast-moving consumer goods industry. And fast-moving it really is!

One year I was in Africa for most of December (yes, we do have factories there too). I thought I'd escape the razzmatazz of Advent expectancy so evident in Oxford Street. But no, the hotel offered piped, syncopated, out-of-tune and slightly slow carols the whole time. In the heat of an African summer's day, tinsel and fake snow hung from an oversized tree. Pre-Christmas fever is one thing, but these experiences jarred!

What a joy it was to escape into the hotel room where, after a busy day on site, I could relax and regain the perspective of what Christmas really means. The coming of the Christ-child can bring peace, God's peace, even to a hectic, international lifestyle like mine.

Getting on the plane home, three days before Christmas, was great: I'd caught a fresh glimpse of the real meaning of Christmas and could return home to share it with the family who were eagerly awaiting my landing.

May each of us know a little more of your righteousness, peace and joy, and your abundant life over this Christmas season.

11 December

'Blessed are the pure in heart, for they will see God.'
MATTHEW 5:8

Seeing God—isn't that what brings us joy? Seeing God in the heart of Christmas, in the heart of anything—our workplace, our families, our neighbourhood—catching a glimpse of his transcendent glory that inspires us to carry on. We can't make it happen. We can't run after joy or force God to reveal himself but, during every Christmas season, there are moments when we see him in the eyes of a five-year-old in the school play, or hear him in the majesty of Christmas music; when we taste something of his goodness through an unexpectedly kind action or catch something of his presence in a news report of people giving up their own Christmas to bring strangers comfort in a war-torn land.

Sometimes he simply chooses to make his presence known to us. One of my most special Christmas moments came when I was about eleven years old and all by myself in the lounge at home one evening. It can't have been my turn to wash up after Boxing Day tea, because that's what my parents and brother were busy doing in the kitchen. All very ordinary—but suddenly I felt God's presence with me—such a warm contentment, such very strong love that I can remember it all these years later.

When we see God, we're not disappointed. When we reach such a depth of worship that we are 'lost in wonder, love and praise', something happens to us and his joy really does become our strength, sustaining us through the mundane. How do we reach that place? There's no complicated formula. Jesus said that the kingdom of heaven belongs to little children, who were drawn to him and loved him because they saw, accepted and responded to his unconditional love for them.

We think of children as pure and innocent—and in some ways they are. But most also have selfishness down to a fine art, along with an inbuilt rebelliousness which constantly tests their boundaries. Original sin is not so much a religious doctrine as a fact that any parent of a two-year-old will recognize.

If our seeing God depended upon a purity that equalled sinless perfection, none of us would ever have the joy of even a tiny glimpse. Just as well, then, that the cleanest things may be those which have been washed the most. Take our lounge chairs, which look best in the places where our baby rabbit had little accidents upon them. The fabric appears bright and good as new on those well-scrubbed and disinfected patches!

To be freshly forgiven brings the joy of experiencing God's saving grace all over again, of having our relationship with him restored, our world transformed. Being pure surely has to do with childlike qualities like saying sorry and accepting forgiveness, of being aware that we can't do things on our own. The pure in heart, along with children who are allowed to be children, know best about wonder and how to enjoy life.

Jodi was nine years old when she was diagnosed with a brain tumour. After treatment, she went into remission and decided to write a booklet to 'give other children courage'. *Jodi's Story** was published just before she died and used in hospitals including the Royal Marsden where she was treated. Typing away on a word processor, Jodi demystified the terrors of hospitals, radiotherapy and a MRI scanner which 'looked like a washing machine and sounded like there were canaries in it'. She wrote honestly of the effects the tumour had on her life at home and school, of the lovely things that happened and all the people who helped her. Finally she wrote:

I might die from this, but it won't matter because heaven is lovely and God is there. I have always believed in God and I know that he is in charge. He is looking after me and he loves me. My favourite Bible story is David and Goliath, because it gives me courage. David was only small and Goliath was huge but he beat him. That is what I want to do, to beat the tumour. Even if it beats me, I don't mind because I'll always be with Jesus. I think heaven is a wonderful, happy place and when you wake up you have a great big golden table with food on it. I think there will be music and dancing and it will be a really fun and happy place, and all the children will be playing around and there will be no school!!!

Lord, may your purity be our priority as your joy gives us strength.

* Copies of *Jodi's Story* may be obtained from St Andrew's Church Parish Office, Church Gate House, Downside Bridge Road, Cobham, Surrey, KT11 3EJ. Send a £2.00 cheque made payable to 'Jodi's Story' to cover postage and packing.

THREE

Love or loneliness?

Introduction

How nice that Carl, her twin brother, had invited them for Christmas. All her family would be there and she and Ben would be able to show off their two-month-old baby girl all over again. Carl had been living in a small flat, but from the description of his new house, Sue reckoned he must be doing quite well for himself suddenly. He even had a lodger, Duncan.

Carl showed them all round as soon as they arrived. 'This is the spare bedroom and this is our bedroom.' The only words that came out of Sue's mouth were, 'Nice curtains!' but her eyes couldn't leave the double bed. Meanwhile, her mind was racing. How could she and Ben have missed the truth? Obviously the rest of the family knew; in fact, they must have known for some time. Yet none of them had mentioned to her or to Ben that her brother was a practising homosexual. Why?

Because they feared their Christian disapproval? What had she said about homosexuality in the past—had she sounded horribly condemning and bigoted? Whatever happened, they couldn't discuss it today! She would have to go downstairs in a minute and pretend to enjoy a nice family Christmas, when she felt as though a bomb had just exploded in her stomach.

Wonderful family Christmases don't always turn out that way. Many people feel hurt or lonely; conflict or rejection can seem particularly sharp at a time of year supposedly oozing with love and goodwill. Yet Jesus' family, left alone in a strange place after the visitors had departed, must have felt the pressure too.

12 December

He was in the world, and the world came into being through him; yet the world did not know him. He came to what was his own, and his own people did not accept him. But to all who received him, who believed in his name, he gave power to become children of God, who were born, not of blood or of the will of the flesh or of the will of man, but of God.

JOHN 1:10–13

Cliff Richard sang about people gathering from far and wide to be together on the 'Saviour's Day'. As people take more time off work, Christmas has become the time to meet up with far-flung family, to catch up with neighbours and to renew old friendships.

All of this must make God happy—families acting as he intended they should, loving and giving and taking delight in one another's pleasure. Generations come together and neighbours call on one another. Seasonal social events in local communities provide opportunities to welcome visitors and newcomers. Old relationships are renewed, if only through a card and a promise to meet up later. Friends show themselves friendly. People keep caring, sharing, giving, and wishing one another well—except, it doesn't always work quite like that.

More people live on their own in this country than ever before. For the rest, we may play 'Happy families' but when a number of people are flung together over Christmas, cracks develop in the seasonal bonhomie and already-strained relationships may break. Counsellors' and divorce solicitors' busiest time of year starts immediately after the Christmas holidays.

Tension in relationships isn't the only problem. It always seems harder at Christmas time when people are missing because of illness or geographical separation. Those who are left often feel bereft and lonely.

From the first mince pie to the last drunken note of 'Auld Lang Syne', the festive season isn't one long party of friendly merry-making. The rejection and alienation that dog so many are not of God's creation but came about as we (plural) walked away from him. Perhaps that is why they applied to Jesus too—forming part of the sacrifice of his atonement as he took on the consequences of our selfishness and alienation. He came to 'his own' and his own people did not accept him. He found no room in Bethlehem, no kingly welcome in Israel, no honour in his own village, nowhere to lay his head. He knew rejection as a healer and as a teacher. Even more, he knew rejection as the Jewish Messiah and as humanity's God and Saviour. He understands what it is like and that is why he longs to include all of us in his own family. Through the final atoning act of dying on the cross and being cut off even from his father, he earned the supernatural right for all of us to become his brothers or sisters—and God's beloved children. All of us who follow him are part of the biggest family on earth.

Duncan Dyason is director of 'The Toybox Charity', a Christian charity helping street children in Latin America. He writes:

Christmas, they say, is a time of giving and receiving. As Christians we have a responsibility to give, in joy and gratitude, for we have freely received from God.

I work with children who themselves have received some of the toughest blows that society can hand out. I am talking about the street children of Guatemala, who have to live on the streets because of abuse or abandonment, or who are runaways from unbelievable home situations. Like Marcos, aged 6, who has been with us for two years. When we found him he was wearing just a pair of shorts, was huddled up on a cold pavement and still today has not been able to express what he went through beforehand.

Despite their traumatized childhood, the children we have managed to rescue off the street have begun to receive love, food, clothing and a home.

This Christmas, the children in our homes have decided to give something back to those they have left behind. They will be going to some very poor areas around Guatemala City and staging Christmas plays, singing songs, handing out small presents that they have bought with their pocket money and sharing how God has changed their lives.

Jesus said, 'Freely you have received, freely give.' I think the children have begun to understand that what we receive is to be enjoyed and shared with those who have nothing.

Father God, we hold up before you today 'The Toybox Charity' and others we know of who help street children or remake family as you intended.

13 December

He grew up before him like a young plant, and like a root out of dry ground; he had no form or majesty that we should look at him, nothing in his appearance that we should desire him. He was despised and rejected by others; a man of suffering and acquainted with infirmity; and as one from whom others hide their faces he was despised, and we held him of no account. Surely he has borne our infirmities and carried our diseases; yet we accounted him stricken, struck down by God, and afflicted. But he was wounded for our transgressions, crushed for our iniquities; upon him was the punishment that made us whole, and by his bruises we are healed.

ISAIAH 53:2–5

Nearly every film or picture of Jesus portrays him with bearded good looks, his eyes hypnotic, not of this world. Often ethereal, his feet hover a centimetre above the ground, his face is pale, hands limp and hair combed and shining, even on the cross.

None of the New Testament writers gives a physical description of Jesus during his earthly ministry. The closest we come is in this passage, which is commonly interpreted as Isaiah prophesying Christ's suffering and death. He goes on to say that onlookers don't even stare, they hide their faces!

What kind of god is this, what kind of hero? Why follow a man known, through Isaiah's prophecies, as the Suffering Servant? The cross stands in opposition to all our culture. To be loved, to gain respect, surely someone must be good-looking, well-clothed and groomed, clean and odour-free, keep on the right side of the law and not upset his mother. He must be popular, retain the loyalty of his friends, wear the right clothes, drive the right car (or chariot) and live in the right neighbourhood surrounded by appropriate status symbols. He must defend himself well, avoid suffering or keep it private, avoid public shame at all costs, accumulate wealth, possessions and fame, achieve great things, and be seen to be having a good, fun time.

Jesus took the opposite view, so who will be first in his kingdom? Maurice West, in his novel *The Clowns of God*, had Jesus come again in the last days of the earth, quietly helping people with Downs Syndrome. Dodgy eschatology perhaps, but truth shines out of the story. Jesus would choose to spend time with such people. He would value them and see those who loved him with all of their hearts as closer to his kingdom than the so-called 'important ones'. When faced with God, none of our trappings, achievements or intellect counts for much: we're simply people that he loves.

Where do we see Jesus—in a polished gold cross carried before a procession of white-robed priests, or in the dark mess of a concentration camp, dying amid blood and sweat on splintered wood?

Dawn, along with fifty other disabled residents, lives and works in a special Centre. I asked how she finds Christmas.

Most people go home to their families, but since Dad died in 1994 I've stayed here. That first year I found it hard to accept that he'd gone and was tearing myself to pieces. The Centre puts on all kinds of Christmas activities for us, but it's not easy, living, working and then socializing with the same people all the time. I've lived here since 1983 and it's worse because I've never felt I had a home. Mum walked out when I was little, leaving Dad to bring up four children while working nights.

I didn't walk till I was thirteen—the doctors said I never would. Water on the brain when I was a baby has left one side of my body weak. After starting at a special boarding school, I never went home for long, even having respite care for the middle two weeks of the summer holidays. I was a difficult add-on who arrived every now and again, rather than part of the family. I couldn't run and sit on Dad's lap like my sister did, I had to crawl. Later I'd visit home but during the last two years of Dad's life he didn't know who I was.

I listen to a Christian radio station before I fall asleep, and one night they talked about how much Father God loves us and longs to wrap his arms around us. That made me cry. Even though church is my real family now, if someone there gives me a hug I go all rigid. I've been a Christian since I was nine, but often I'll push God away or hide from him. He always seeks me out, though, he's so patient. It's taken me a long while to trust that he really loves me, that he will 'never leave me nor forsake me'. Last year, standing by the sea at Margate, I was able to let go of Dad, to forgive him, which is the hardest thing—even though I understand now what a difficult time he had.

I still have my good and bad days, though. Living here, things can easily upset me. I know that every day I need to trust God and let him take control. And church helps—not just sitting there but, for example, taking my turn leading worship in house group on Wednesday nights. Although I'll maybe never achieve my ambition of working with children (I'm not strong enough to pick them up), I love helping with the crèche at church once a month and feel I'm helping the children get used to someone with a disability. I've come to understand that, though I may be different on the outside, in God's family we're all the same inside.

Jesus, you suffered rejection in order that we might be included in your family. May those who feel alone know your comfort today and your flesh and blood family too, drawing close to them.

14 December

They made his grave with the wicked and his tomb with the rich, although he had done no violence, and there was no deceit in his mouth. Yet it was the will of the Lord to crush him with pain. When you make his life an offering for sin, he shall see his offspring, and shall prolong his days; through him the will of the Lord shall prosper. Out of his anguish he shall see light; he shall find satisfaction through his knowledge. The righteous one, my servant, shall make many righteous, and he shall bear their iniquities. Therefore I will allot him a portion with the great, and he shall divide the spoil with the strong; because he poured out himself to death, and was numbered with the transgressors; yet he bore the sin of many, and made intercession for the transgressors.

Isaiah 53:9–12

It's terrible to see anyone crushed with the kind of pain that reduces them, squeezing everything else out, as agony becomes their prison, their universe. How unimaginable that Jesus, 'God with us', was crushed with pain at all levels—physical, emotional, spiritual—until finally the most vibrant life that ever lived cried, 'It is finished!' Yet, centuries before Jesus' birth, Isaiah prophesies not only his death but his resurrection. All that suffering, that crushing, brought light and 'satisfaction' in an amazing way. It reversed the effects of evil, 'making many righteous'. It was finished all right, but in a way that brought real hope, not despair.

Some things weren't finished, though. His first coming didn't do away with suffering here on earth. Perhaps that is just as well, for suffering schools us. If all Christians lived charmed, trouble-free lives, we wouldn't help this world much. I know of a Christian woman who did commendable work helping others, yet her brisk, hard edge alienated many. Twenty years later she has become much more human, showing real understanding and empathy. What changed her? The suicide of her son.

But people faced with the isolation of crushing pain find words trite—and Christmas jollity may magnify and mock their suffering. Perhaps a more real comfort is that Jesus has been there—and not 'just' in the comparatively brief hours before his death. Growing up in a world without antibiotics or inoculations, some of Jesus' playmates from Nazareth would have died—their parents too. God allowed his Son to be born into a world where Herod could order the deaths of babies simply because they had been born in the wrong place at the wrong time. When the Romans crucified three men on Good Friday, that was an unusually small number. At the least suspicion of rebellion, they would line the roads into Jerusalem with crosses, crucifying hundreds.

With human life cheap and human suffering too commonplace to raise a headline, no Convention on Human Rights challenged them, no United Nations troops flew to the rescue. Jesus really was a 'man of suffering and acquainted with infirmity' and yet the letter to the Hebrews says that he loved righteousness and hated wickedness; therefore God anointed him with the oil of gladness beyond his companions.

Single and in her early 50s, Pauline Clackson is a counsellor and ex-social worker. She has felt crushed with pain, which came to a head with the destruction of some crib figurines. She writes:

The little olive wood statues were smooth and warm to my touch, their faces showing serenity and joy. It was difficult to choose which set to buy all those years ago, as I stood in the crowded shop in Bethlehem, examining the wonderfully carved crib figures, but I took the set which had first attracted me, paying for it with my hard-earned holiday money.

Every year, a week before Christmas, I lovingly unpacked each figure, and set up the scene—a poignant reminder of my unforgettable holiday in Israel.

It was a ritual that, on returning from the Christmas Eve midnight service, I would place the tiny carved baby Jesus in his mother's arms and think of the love of a mother for her child.

Two years ago my mother stayed with me over Christmas, and shared in the task of putting up the decorations, the tree and the setting up of the crib. She stayed with my sister for New Year and on 5 January she died, two days after returning to her flat. The emptiness I had felt on the death of my father, three years previously, was magnified a thousandfold. I felt lost and abandoned.

During the time between Mother's death and her funeral, I hastily took down the gaudy decorations and synthetic tree and packed the wooden crib into its box, shoving them all into black plastic bags. I left them in a corner to sort out later but, when I returned from the nightmare of the funeral, the corner was bare. My cleaner had taken all the 'rubbish' to the tip. Not only had I lost both my parents, but those things which linked me with times of joy and happiness—those symbols of Jesus, the tools of my Christmas ritual.

The following year, hoping a complete change would do me good, I booked a Christmas holiday in a Cyprus hotel. What with non-stop rain and the fact I didn't feel like celebrating, it proved a difficult experience. However, a fellow guest planned a trip to Israel during the holiday. I felt sure he would be visiting Bethlehem so, after telling him this story, I asked him to find me a crib. On the evening of his return, as we sat round the dinner table, he presented me with a large box from the same shop in Bethlehem which I had visited so many years before. In joyful anticipation I opened it. Inside lay olive wood carved statues, smooth and warm to my touch, their faces full of serenity and joy. What a gift from an understanding God! They were even better than the ones I'd lost. As my hands caressed the carvings, my eyes flooded with tears—it was exactly a year to that very hour that my mother had died.

Thank you, Jesus, that you live to make intercession for us.

15 December

Sing, O barren one who did not bear; burst into song and shout, you who have not been in labour! For the children of the desolate woman will be more than the children of her that is married, says the Lord. Enlarge the site of your tent, and let the curtains of your habitations be stretched out; do not hold back; lengthen your cords and strengthen your stakes. For you will spread out to the right and to the left, and your descendants will possess the nations and will settle the desolate towns.

ISAIAH 54:1–3

It's hard for us to imagine the shame and disgrace that childless women of Old Testament times would feel. Desolate, with no one to care for them in their old age, they were regarded as cursed by God. Contradicting that notion strongly, here God promises teeming life from barrenness, hope from despair and blesses those who feel cursed.

Today some people choose the childless option while others, striving for a family by every means, face long-drawn-out disappointment if no babies come. Christian women outnumber Christian men and many, not wanting to marry unbelievers, will remain single and childless. That's hard, especially at Christmas time when much is made of children—from advertising and TV schedules to the family services held in most churches on Christmas morning. Apart from children's work and coffee rotas, the only role open to a woman in some churches may be to lead a house-group—with her husband. Pastoral care and discipleship focus on the 'standard' family with 2.4 children, and most social events, other than for teens and twenties, are designed for couples or families.

Yet God affirms and cares about single people and childless couples. He wants to bless them and enlarge their sphere and ministry; he wants them to sing and to be heard; he wants them to bless and to restore others. So, consider people who, for whatever reason, feel desolate and barren at times. They have so much to give (and not just baby-sitting, either!)

Margery Denne is enjoying an active retirement but used to be Head of a physically handicapped unit within a mainstream infant school. An only child, she's never married, but is an outgoing person. I wondered how her Christmases have been. Her eyes lit up.

You know, I always longed for big, family Christmases. Since my childhood I'd always spent them with my parents, just the three of us. I loved my parents dearly, but as they grew older they'd doze off after lunch and I'd imagine everyone else in big parties, enjoying themselves. Thank heavens for TV! I'd be invited out but couldn't leave them at that stage. I loved church on Christmas morning but otherwise was glad when the festivities were over and things returned to normal.

They died thirteen years ago and my great friend from college days invited me to stay with her family over Christmas. Anne and her clergyman husband, Ernest, lived with their nearly grown-up children in a huge Essex rectory. I stayed with them five years running and we had enormous fun, but still… everything was done for me. I didn't bother with a tree or decorations at home.

One year my neighbour asked if I would keep an eye on her house while she was away over Christmas. Ernest had retired by then. He and Anne had bought a much smaller house, their three children had married and there were grandchildren. Anne insisted that I should still visit—but with me occupying one bedroom, they could have only one family to stay at a time. I phoned her. 'How would you feel about coming to me instead? I'll ask my neighbour if we could use her house too, so there would be plenty of room.' Anne's initial doubts vanished when my neighbour said she'd be delighted— and all Anne's children's families said they'd love to come.

So for the first time ever, I strung decorations all around my home, bought a huge turkey and an enormous Christmas tree. Eight adults plus four grandchildren stayed several nights. Ernest did most of the cooking. Knowing I'm no chef, they'd only let me prepare the Brussels sprouts! We played silly games and the excited children opened their presents under the tree. As Christians, they put God at the centre of everything, so it was all I'd ever hoped for. The next Christmas, they all wanted to come again, and the one after. There'll be seven grandchildren this year. It may be the last at my place as one of the families has bought a holiday cottage—and that's fine. Whatever happens in the future, my memories no longer centre around a hidey-hole of nothingness, but the Christmases of my dreams—joyful, if exhausting, times!

Father God, may all those who feel lonely and desolate this Christmas know an end to their barrenness.

16 December

Do not fear, for you will not be ashamed; do not be discouraged, for you will not suffer disgrace; for you will forget the shame of your youth, and the disgrace of your widowhood you will remember no more. For your Maker is your husband, the Lord of Hosts is his name; the Holy One of Israel is your Redeemer, the God of the whole earth he is called. For the Lord has called you like a wife forsaken and grieved in spirit, like the wife of a man's youth when she is cast off, says your God... with everlasting love I will have compassion on you, says the Lord, your Redeemer.

ISAIAH 54:4–6, 8

Shame and disgrace are words so powerful that we don't like to look at them too closely. We'll talk about guilt and forgiveness because they are at the heart of the gospel. Yet look at the doubts cast on the legitimacy of Jesus' birth. His own village said, 'Can any good come out of Nazareth?' He was mocked and he died, between thieves, spreadeagled naked on the cross, with no way of hiding his unimaginable suffering. It's clear that while guilt is associated with sin, shame and disgrace need not be.

This passage mentions the disgrace of widowhood. Some things do change for the better! While today's widows (and widowers) sometimes put up with a lot, at least our society doesn't heap disgrace on their heads. But, for whatever reason we feel shame, it has negative effects on our lives. Some disqualify themselves from many activities because their education was cut short. Others still believe childhood put-downs: 'You're stupid... lazy... no good.' Abuse and bullying leave shame so deep that it can drive to suicide. Shame can silence, or make us over-talkative; it can make us avoid certain people or situations; it can make us desperate for signs of acceptance from others because we're too ashamed to accept ourselves.

Jesus knows all about shame and disgrace and can deal with them. Though we do things which make him angry, his love for us is everlasting. He is never ashamed of the person we are—the person he made us to be. 'Do not be discouraged,' he says, when we are at our lowest. He knows all about us and our shame, secret or open, 'deserved' or not. Still he loves and accepts us. He wants us to get to know him better—and to extend to the frail human beings whom we meet the same compassion and comfort that he gives to us.

Pat Davidson's husband left her quite suddenly in 1986, after 21 years of what had been a very companionable marriage. I asked her what had happened and how she had felt.

We'd just come back from a holiday in Switzerland. I thought he'd been behaving oddly for about three weeks; now I recognize that his behaviour changed about six months before. He was the nicest, kindest man. He'd do anything for anyone and although he was never the affectionate type, we had a very full and happy life together. So when he announced that he'd come home to our flat merely to collect a few things—that he was staying with a 'mate' and wanted a divorce—I couldn't believe it. Later I found that he wanted to marry his dancing teacher, an older woman. I felt numb. It was the last thing I thought would happen. We had no children and I've always hated being alone. I'd wake up in the middle of the night, my heart pounding! The worst part was the loneliness. I had no family and few close friends—we'd done everything together, you see.

I tried to keep in touch. He left me in the September and though I asked if I'd see him over Christmas he never sent word. In the end, my neighbour's daughter invited me to her house on Christmas Day. It wasn't the happiest time of my life but I got through it. You have to. He remarried only a few weeks after our divorce was made absolute.

My elderly neighbour was so upset by what had happened. She was crying and I was crying. She wondered if her church minister might help. I'd not been to church for years, but I thought, yes, it would be good to talk with someone right outside of the situation. It was, too. Before he left, the minister asked if he could pray with me and I found myself saying I'd like to go to church—I can't think why, except that I felt so rejected and he said I'd be very welcome. Though I wouldn't even go into a café for a cup of tea on my own, I went along the next Sunday—and cried the whole way through the service. People were ever so kind, and I went twice more, but that church wasn't 'me' somehow. So I took myself—all on my own again—to the parish church across the road, and it's become my life. I'm sacristan there now—a responsible job. I have to set everything out, just so. I go to all the services and make sure everything is ready. I'm a tidy, organized person and I love it, even the midweek services when hardly anyone's there. I'm on the evangelism committee too. As for being lonely, so many good church friends treat me as part of their families. They vie with each other as to who'll invite me for Christmas or Easter, or for Sunday lunch and tea!

I'm convinced God had his hand in what I was doing all the way through. Why else would I have acted so out of character in going to two different churches all on my own? I tell people, 'God is there for you. You may ignore him for years but he waits patiently on the sidelines.' He certainly took care of me. I don't know where I'd be now without him. I pray to him all day. I don't always feel his presence: sometimes it's really a discipline to keep praying—but I know that he's always faithful and always there.

For those who feel ashamed, Lord, be their glory; for those who feel lonely, may they find you—and us—to be true friends.

17 December

'Blessed are the merciful, for they will receive mercy.'
MATTHEW 5:7

Mercy—not a word we think about much. It sounds condescending, like one of those Victorian virtues—'charity' or 'pity'. Yet Shakespeare wrote one of his most lyrical pieces on mercy, spoken by Portia:

> *The quality of mercy is not strained.*
> *It droppeth as the gentle rain from heaven*
> *Upon the place beneath. It is twice blest;*
> *It blesseth him that gives, and him that takes.*
> *'Tis mightiest in the mightiest. It becomes*
> *The thronèd monarch better than his crown...*
> *It is an attribute to God himself,*
> *And earthly power doth then show likest God's*
> *When mercy seasons justice.*
> THE MERCHANT OF VENICE, ACT 4 SCENE 1

I don't know about you, but plenty of people have shown me mercy— my parents, my husband, my children, my friends, my church, my workmates. The giving and receiving of forgiveness, the proving of unconditional love, make relationships stronger and allow room for growth, despite wrongdoing and mistakes.

Mercy is about grace, showing favour where it's not deserved. It's about forgiveness and generosity. I used to think that forgiving someone meant twisting things round in your mind so that the wrong action didn't seem wrong any more. In fact, of course, it's about releasing all that is best for a person even though his/her deed or word was wrong. It's about allowing God to release us from the hurt before our anger hardens to form a bitter plug, which blocks the flow of his unending love.

Grace, generosity, forgiveness—as human beings we receive them daily from God. Not weak qualities, they're as strong and vital as rain is to the earth. And like 'the gentle rain from heaven', which plants take into themselves, then transpire back to the clouds, there is a cycle: we receive mercy as we give it; our sins are forgiven as we forgive others. Anything else would lead to a desert barren of relationships, like sisters who haven't spoken since one upset the other thirty Christmases ago.

We may not bear grudges, but might like to consider how we can show generosity and grace this Christmas-time towards those who don't necessarily deserve or have a right to it from us.

Sandra and Jonathan Snell live with their four children on the Isle of Wight, where Jonathan is a church minister and Sandra runs a playgroup. Sandra told me:

Living on the Island, we don't very often have relatives to stay over Christmas, but I enjoy cooking and giving hospitality, so I keep my eyes open for anyone on their own. A couple of weeks beforehand, I'll invite them round. It might be a single mum with two teenage daughters or an older man who's alone—not necessarily church people—anyone I notice, really. If it's Christmas Day, they might join us for the morning service. Some prefer not to, but they all come to our house for lunch and presents.

'That's quite something when you have four children!' I commented. 'How old are they—and what do they make of strangers joining you for Christmas?'

At the moment our children range between six and eighteen. They've always been pretty good, and we do keep either Christmas or Boxing Day as a special time for just our family. They see another perspective, though, when we include others in. After all, Christmas is a time for sharing!

'How did it all start?' I asked.

Twelve years ago we lived in Winchester. We invited all the neighbours round for coffee and mince pies and got to know them. One family became good friends and started coming to church regularly. In fact, they still go to our old church. That's how we started our tradition of keeping 'open house' for one day over the Christmas holiday. But having someone round either Christmas or Boxing Day really began in this house, when I noticed people on their own. I didn't think it would become something we'd do most years—but that's what happened. I'd say we enjoy Christmas all the more as a family because we share it with others.

Thank you, God, for your grace, for your mercy, for the way you reach out and include us. Thank you for those who have shown those same qualities to us. (*You might like to stop and think about specific examples.*) Show us how we can do the same for others this Christmas season and in the year to come.

FOUR

Peace or pain?

Introduction

Quiet (or strife-torn), dark times come to all of us sometimes, taking many forms—illness, grief, family pain, fear, depression... Sometimes these dark times affect our personal peace, sometimes that of a group or of society as a whole. In an occupied country, bored shepherds, huddled together against the cold, suddenly found one of their nights transformed into something majestic and holy. Sadly, that doesn't always happen—not with such drama, anyway!

But I'm thinking of a church whose leader became out of touch. It entered a painful time during which gifts were not encouraged and the congregation became confused and fragmented. They chose different places to hide rather than adding fuel to the fire or risking getting burnt. Once the leader had moved on, roles were gradually rediscovered and relationships re-established. The church recovered a sense of tolerance and community—and then the talents began to appear. For example, some people decided to decorate the church for the millennial Christmas, making a crib and exuberant wall-hangings to remind them how Jesus came into the world, as well as numerous stars to symbolize hope and guidance. They struggled to form fiddly lengths of basket-cane into star shapes. They made plenty of mistakes as they learnt to work with cloth and wire and wood and wax—and discovered plenty of new talents too. They drank coffee and laughed together and, as each helped another, they forgot the pain of rheumatic fingers and of strained relationships. They not only created a beautifully decorated church that Christmas, but found that God used their efforts to help re-create an even more beautiful church-full of people.

18 December

And the Word became flesh and lived among us, and we have seen his glory, the glory as of a father's only son, full of grace and truth.

JOHN 1:14

Glory is not necessarily peaceful. According to the *Concise Oxford Dictionary*, it means, 'Exalted renown, honourable fame… resplendent majesty, beauty or magnificence, effulgence of heavenly light…'. How did John and his friends see Jesus' glory as he lived among them on this earth?

Words like 'fame', 'honour' and 'resplendence' aren't, at first sight, suited to the baby in the manger, though glory did break through, for those who had eyes to see. Foreigners made their mysterious way across eastern deserts, their costly gifts of scant use to anyone but a dying king. Bethlehem's dark skies could no longer contain the choirs of angels trumpeting the rejoicing of heaven. But that rejoicing didn't come easy, either in heaven or on earth.

What were God's feelings when he sent his only Son to a planet whose inhabitants had destroyed previous messengers? Or of the foreign stargazers who, in seeking the Prince of Peace, sparked a massacre of children? Did their glorious encounter leave them, like Mary (Luke 1:28–29), greatly blessed and greatly troubled for the rest of their lives?

Jesus' pain-filled road led to ascension and victory, to the veil of the temple being torn in two and the re-establishment of a bridgehead between heaven and earth. Some saw his glory established when, within a human frame, he held together on this earth grace and truth—unconditional love and uncompromising holiness. As Psalm 85 says, 'Surely his salvation is at hand for those who fear him, that his glory may dwell in our land. Steadfast love and faithfulness will meet; righteousness and peace will kiss each other.'

To his followers Jesus promised both peace and pain. At Christmas the white, pure candles, the royal colours, the sumptuous generosity of the feasting—all these things come with a price. God's glory, peace and joy are not shiny wrapping paper, taped over a throwaway gift. They encompass his grace and truth in a world marred by selfishness, greed, pain and war. Jesus' birth did reveal God's glory and the beginnings of peace between heaven and humanity. That's why it causes us even now to wonder and to worship—if we have eyes to see.

Fay Sampson writes novels for children and adults, and books on church history. She lives in a Devon village, in a 16th-century cottage on a hillside above a farm. She writes about wonder:

I love everything about Christmas—mixing the puddings and leaving the huge bowl on the kitchen table so that everyone can make a wish (no more magical than any other prayer, but it concentrates the mind on what is the one thing I really, really want to happen this year); buying presents for the people I love; carols and candlelight; the family home together to keep the festival.

But I believe in Advent. Many festive preparations I leave as late as possible. Just before the family arrive, I scour the garden and hedgerows for evergreens and weave them through garlands of silver and gold to loop from the oak beams. On the afternoon of Christmas Eve I am in my kitchen, making dozens of mince pies as I listen to the carols from King's College chapel. In snatched moments I wrap the presents and smuggle them downstairs to set around the Christmas tree. (I had to be weaned from the pillowcase on the end of my bed when my own children outgrew this.) And then there are advance preparations for the huge Christmas dinner, part traditional, part innovative, perhaps with an exotic stuffing that will double as a main course for vegetarians.

It's nearly done. I'm as excited as a child, waiting for the transformation of my world tomorrow. And tomorrow is almost here. In the city centre, groups of revellers stand on the street corners or outside bars. We Christians light our torches and walk through the trafficless streets carolling the good news. Half an hour before midnight, we reach an open church and our service begins. Christ is born. We turn and greet each other. It is Christmas Day.

Yet I still wake early. Miraculously, no one else is stirring. This is my chance to steal downstairs for a quiet breakfast and get through all those things which still need to be done, so that I too have time to relax and enjoy people. I walk into the kitchen, in the first light of a winter sunrise. The neighbour's field comes right up to my window. I see a sheep, quite close, panting in the cold air. I hold my breath as I realize what her efforts mean. I am only just in time. I watch the slick, black sac slip from her loins to lie curled on the grass. She turns and licks it, lovingly. It squirms and staggers, stands shakily upright, fumbles for her teat.

A lamb was born on Christmas Day, and I was there to see it.

'And we beheld his glory.'

Lord, may we rest in your peace in good times—and in times of painful turmoil see the glory through the grey.

19 December

'Peace I leave with you; my peace I give to you. I do not give to you as the world gives. Do not let your hearts be troubled, and do not let them be afraid.'
JOHN 14:27

Jesus has just spent the first part of this chapter telling the disciples that he is going to leave them. He knows he is going to a terrible death. Being dragged before various authorities, flogged, mocked and put to death is not a peaceful experience. Jesus was in such agony of spirit that, even before the events began, he was sweating great drops of blood. I'm so pleased he wasn't singing, 'I'm happy, clappy happy and all is peace and light, My God is always good to me, makes everything all right!'

Can he really expect his disciples to prevent their hearts being troubled, when he himself is described as 'troubled in spirit' (John 13:21)? It's all very well Jesus (and the rest of the Bible) telling us not to fear and not to worry. On occasions when our troubled minds and spirits whirl around like demented food-processors, how can he add that secret ingredient of the peace that is beyond understanding?

Letting go of the one to receive the other isn't easy: if it were, we wouldn't have to be told so many times! Believe me, as one whose overactive worrying mechanism can spin me into all kinds of trouble, I know what I'm talking about. But when that peace does come through the pain or the worry or the fear, we know it's from him and are filled with awe. After he's walked with us through the valley of the shadow, he invites us to a banquet in the presence of our enemies. He tells the disciples, in John 16:20, 'Very truly, I tell you, you will weep and mourn, but the world will rejoice; you will have pain, but your pain will turn into joy.'

Peace or pain?

Joy Carroll is an Anglican priest. She ministered for ten years in inner-city churches of South London and for the last two has lived in Washington DC with her husband, Jim Wallis, and son Luke. She writes:

Being a priest means sharing in people's joy and in their pain. Christmas can be a painful time for people who are lonely or alone; for people who are sick or caring for someone sick; for those unable to have children and those who can't afford to give their children special things; for those without homes or those with mortgages that can't be paid; for those living in war zones or suffering from the effects of poverty. Christmas is especially hard for those who grieve the loss of someone they loved.

Christmas has become far too sanitized and quite unrelated to God's dramatic entry into human history—a vulnerable baby, born to an unmarried mother, in a filthy barn. Lowly shepherds first heard the news that Christ was born. If we want to find God's peace this Christmas, perhaps we should seek out some of those who are in pain for one reason or another. God has a habit of being there. It's the nature of God incarnate. But life is also fun at times and God laughs with us. I really enjoyed watching the 'Vicar of Dibley' TV series emerge, having helped writer Richard Curtis develop the character—a truly human woman priest who cried and laughed with the odd parishioners that surrounded her. Laughing priests are a very good thing.

O God, the source of all good desires, all right judgments, and all just works: give to your servants that peace which the world cannot give; that our hearts may be set to obey your commandments, and that freed from fear of our enemies, we may pass our time in rest and quietness; through Jesus Christ our Lord.

COLLECT FOR PEACE (ASB)

20 December

A shoot shall come out from the stump of Jesse, and a branch shall grow out of his roots. The spirit of the Lord shall rest on him, the spirit of wisdom and understanding, the spirit of counsel and might, the spirit of knowledge and the fear of the Lord. His delight shall be in the fear of the Lord. He shall not judge by what his eyes see, or decide by what his ears hear; but with righteousness he shall judge the poor, and decide with equity for the meek of the earth; he shall strike the earth with the rod of his mouth, and with the breath of his lips he shall kill the wicked. Righteousness shall be the belt around his waist, and faithfulness the belt around his loins.

Isaiah 11:1–5

What an amazing description of the character of Jesus, who came among us at Christmas! There are enough clues in the Old Testament as to the qualities of the person God would send as his Messiah ('Anointed One'): a suffering servant who defends the weak; a king who, as Psalm 45 says, rides out on behalf of truth, humility and justice—not just for individuals but for society! If we all put ourselves under his rule, there would be peace on earth; goodwill would flow from God to all humankind.

His is not the kind of power that crushes. Isaiah 60:17 says, 'I will appoint Peace as your overseer and Righteousness as your taskmaster.' How different from the treatment Israel experienced from the slave-masters in Egypt! Jesus never imposes or uses coercion.

Though he brought the characteristics outlined in today's Bible passage to earth, do people still follow him and seek to live in the same way, showing the same attitudes, caring about people, establishing peace and the rule of God? Yes, they do. I know, as I'm sure you do, Christians on whom the Spirit of the Lord rests, even if not all the time. We just know that their wisdom and understanding, their ability to give wise counsel, comes from God. Some act in ways which show they respect God more than anything or anyone else.

Wondering how Jesus' Spirit can bring wisdom and understanding, peace and new life to someone in very real pain, I talked to Kathleen Simmonds, a lively woman in her early 70s. Her marriage of over 43 years ended with her husband's death on 2 January 1993. I asked her if his death had been unexpected.

Not really; he'd been in and out of hospital for a while. He'd been knocked down by a speeding motorist after visiting a backslidden Christian from our church and, though he survived the accident, he needed twelve operations for broken bones. Alan had done such a lot in church and they prayed for him every Sunday. When he was able to stagger around with a stick and help with communion again, everyone was so pleased, but soon he was complaining of stomach pains and having a liver biopsy. When the specialist told him the cancer was incurable, Alan decided he wanted to spend his last month at home.

People in the church said it wasn't fair and why was God treating him like that? But Alan didn't see it that way and nor did I. He accepted it, writing all his own cards, to former colleagues and old friends, telling them that this would be his last Christmas. He got dressed each day and sat by the phone, which kept on ringing. People were so surprised when he answered it. He said he was able to talk about eternal things to non-Christians more in that month than in the whole of the rest of his life. People arrived to see him, looking worried, and they came out blessed. They'd invariably give me a hug as they left. We'd have a little cry together and then I'd mop my eyes before I went back to him.

A doctor would visit each day and, as well as giving medical treatment, would pray for us. The GPs in our practice are all Christians and they were so good. Of course it was a sad time but at least all our children and grandchildren could be there. Our daughter Heather's birthday falls on New Year's Eve and her 40th was the last time Alan sat at the dinner-table. He wore his dinner jacket, though he couldn't eat anything by then. He died peacefully in his sleep two days later. Afterwards all the family came to see him and young Steven said, 'Grandad's asleep but he's not breathing.' Most of them accepted his death, but the youngest, Andrew, grieved for quite a while.

Alan was a good man. There was standing room only at the funeral. In the end, though, you've got to get on with life, haven't you? Alan had always done the garden but that spring I thought I'd better tidy it up. To my surprise I found gardening very therapeutic, especially when working in the front, because people would stop and talk. In the end my daughter put up a notice warning, 'Trespassers will be chatted to'. I arranged to get help in the house because it was better to spend time with people than indoors all alone!

Anniversaries were hard at first. In fact, one of the grandchildren asked, 'Are we going to be sad every 2nd January at 8.45?' Even a couple of years ago, on that date, though I wasn't consciously thinking about it I found myself in floods of tears in church as I took communion. But I try now to do positive, happy things—for example, I buy a new shrub for the garden each year on Alan's birthday. And this year, on what would have been our golden wedding, I bought myself a gold cross and chain 'from Alan' and treated all the family out for a meal. I have a good life. I've lots of friends, and my church too. God's good.

I'd got to know Kathleen on a Mediterranean holiday, when she gamely joined a series of workshops I was running on creative writing. Her evident enjoyment of life, her willingness to try (and succeed) at new things, her love for her friends and family, and her straight-forward, everyday faith, spoke to me of what the Lord can do with someone who is meek and fears him—someone who lets him lead them with righteousness and faithfulness, with wisdom and under-standing, out of pain and into peace.

Lord, may we become more like you in spirit.

21 December

The wolf shall live with the lamb, the leopard shall lie down with the kid, the calf and the lion and the fatling together, and a little child shall lead them. The cow and the bear shall graze, their young shall lie down together; and the lion shall eat straw like the ox. The nursing child shall play over the hole of the asp, and the weaned child shall put its hand on the adder's den. They will not hurt or destroy on all my holy mountain; for the earth will be full of the knowledge of the Lord as the waters cover the sea. On that day the root of Jesse shall stand as a signal to the peoples; the nations shall inquire of him, and his dwelling shall be glorious.

Isaiah 11:6–10

It's a wonderful picture. It should rank up there alongside Noah's Ark in children's activity or crayoning books, except that, well, it isn't a story. We're not told how it's going to happen. And it hasn't happened. We're not all peaceful vegetarians, even in church! And as for Jerusalem, whose name means 'Possession of Peace', throughout the ages it has remained a place where tensions boil over, setting off no end of trouble. Worldwide, more people are Christians now than at any point in history, but the knowledge of the Lord is far from covering the earth as the waters cover the sea. Jesus, the root or descendant of David's father Jesse, did stand as a signal to the peoples. Many people enquire of him, some make his dwelling glorious, through their lives and art—but not all rulers, not all peoples look to him, not by a long way.

The picture may be for the future, following Christ's second advent, or second coming—pie in the sky when we die. Or perhaps it takes us full circle back to the plan of the earth as God intended it, before the selfish desire of human beings to go their own way spoilt everything and introduced suffering, death and 'nature red in tooth and claw'. Imagine lions on God's new, redeemed earth eating straw and reverse-evolving their jaws to resemble those of cows. Imagine snakes, free of venom and constriction, becoming wiggly playthings for children.

Maybe we can help it happen, making mini 'mountains of the Lord' where enemies can meet in peace and safety—not warring Jewish and Arab leaders, perhaps, but people in our community, our family, our church, even. My daughter was investigating an A-Level in sociology, but backed away when the tutor mentioned the need for an interest in current affairs. 'Watching the news makes me cry,' she confessed to me at home—and I know what she means. So as television brings into our homes disturbing images of violence and enmity, let's use Isaiah's picture to give us hope, lifting us out of the blackness and lending us faith as we pray!

Grandfather John Breeze is enjoying a busy retirement from his job as tutor radiographer. As well as sharing hobbies like caravanning with his wife, he is involved in local and Christian broadcasting and works occasionally with the Garden Tomb (Jerusalem) Association as a guide. He spent Christmas 1993 in Israel and writes:

Jerusalem's Christchurch lounge was packed for an informal Christmas service. Some Palestinian Christians were sharing experiences of what it is like living in late 20th-century Bethlehem. Rejected by their fellow Muslim Palestinians because they were Christian 'Infidels!' and under suspicion from the Israelis because they were Palestinians, they had to carry identity cards wherever they went. There had been recent terrorist attacks in Jerusalem. Because of the security situation, their movements were very severely restricted and they were subject to frequent searches. Yet here in this small enclave, this little fellowship, there was a sense of the reality of the kingdom of God. In the assembled group a dozen nationalities were represented, as different in character as calf and lion. Yet here they were sitting together and showing love, care and concern for these young Christians. At least here Isaiah's dream was being fulfilled!

I bind unto myself today
The power of God to hold and lead,
His eye to watch, his might to stay,
His ear to hearken to my need,
The wisdom of my God to teach,
His hand to guide, his shield to ward,
The word of God to give me speech,
His heavenly host to be my guard.

FROM AN ANCIENT HYMN ATTRIBUTED TO ST PATRICK (385–464),
TRANS. CECIL FRANCES ALEXANDER (1818–95)

22 December

In that region there were shepherds living in the fields, keeping watch over their flock by night. Then an angel of the Lord stood before them, and the glory of the Lord shone around them, and they were terrified. But the angel said to them, 'Do not be afraid; for see—I am bringing you good news of great joy for all the people: to you is born this day in the city of David a Saviour, who is the Messiah, the Lord. This will be a sign for you: you will find a child wrapped in bands of cloth and lying in a manger.' And suddenly there was with the angel a multitude of the heavenly host, praising God and saying, 'Glory to God in the highest heaven, and on earth peace among those whom he favours!'

LUKE 2:8–14

After being brought face to face with the *shekinah* glory surrounding God, those rough shepherds lived to tell the tale, hurrying to see Mary, Joseph and the baby, making 'known what had been told them about this child'. Then we hear no more except that they 'returned, glorifying and praising God for all they had heard and seen'.

Was it peaceful afterwards, back there in the fields with the sheep? Was life ever the same for them again? Maybe it was. Maybe it became too peaceful and they settled back into the old routines, opting to push to the back of their minds that startling moment when eternity broke into the everyday existence of 'ordinary' people.

For the shepherds, a quiet, dark time did become, for a while, the holiest of nights, but it doesn't always. Neither before nor after the birth of Jesus has God always brought peace to the ordinary people of this earth, or to 'those whom he favours'. To Peter, the rock on whom he said he would build his Church, he promised that 'when you grow old, you will stretch out your hands, and someone else will fasten a belt around you and take you where you do not wish to go' (John 21:18). Paul knew floggings, shipwrecks, prison and most likely execution in Rome. John suffered exile on the harsh island of Patmos. Yet all experienced peace with God on earth—and now share in his glory.

Let's think about what the promise of the angel's song means for us, today. We may not be facing martyrdom—but equally Christmas, for all the hype, is hardly the most peaceful time of year. It's also a time when any pain in our lives causes us extra grief.

Elaine Crutchley works as a child psychiatrist in a busy family centre. She writes:

Working with young people and their families can often mean entering into the pain experienced by so many as they struggle with fear, low self-worth, abandonment. It is all too easy to focus too exclusively on the darker side of humanity, but I have found that even in these darker situations suddenly the peace of God can burst into an apparently unredeemable situation. Suddenly God seems to give the situation a totally different dimension, and the grip of depression is loosened. For me, these moments are very special, often lit up by laughter, by the shared discovery of this new way of being alive, of rediscovery of relationships which had lost their meaning. Bethlehem is no longer a drab, ordinary place but the centre of God's earth-shattering plan for humanity!

In recent months I have been aware of this in my personal life as well. As a professional, focusing on other people's lives, it is all too easy to minimize or ignore painful issues in my own. This pain could not be ignored, however: my mother was dying from cancer. I started to put my thoughts down on paper as I sat by Mum's bed. She had slipped into a coma, our last words had been said and there was nothing more I could do. Somehow there I became aware of God's peace as I reflected on how the veil between earth and heaven was being pulled aside for Mum. She had been so aware of an angelic presence on the night before she lost consciousness. Not a mighty host, but a little boy sitting at the end of her bed and a capacity to see loved ones that were beyond my earthbound vision. God brings us peace in pain in his own inimitable way!

Father, help all who suffer in this upside-down world, and also those who strive that your justice and your compassion may be incarnate here.

23 December

'Blessed are the peacemakers, for they will be called children of God.'
MATTHEW 5:9

Think of children and the word 'peacemakers' doesn't always spring to mind! Some Christmases, after mine received all kinds of presents and sweets, watched some fine TV, played with their new bike or games and then squabbled endlessly, I felt like banging their heads together and locking them in their bedrooms with no supper. Perhaps more politically correct remedies occur to you!

Occasionally, though, a child will pour oil on troubled waters, will reconcile the group to the outsider or one faction with another. I remember one or two children like that at school. If they saw an unhappy person, they would try to make things better. For small people it's an unusual gift but can occur, even in three-year-olds. And, of course, children can help ease tensions in a family. Simply by being there, they remind everyone of what is really important.

Christians are children of God, adopted into his family. But are we peaceful? Of course we often get things wrong, but statistics indicate that churchgoers have fewer psychiatric problems and marriage break-ups, are happier, healthier and live longer than those with no religion.

We work actively for peace, too. Few are diplomats by profession but most of us pray for international situations. We give money to relief and development organizations which promote peace and well-being. Some of us make peace where we live or work, bringing 'positive opposites' to replace the aggression, isolation and mistrust which are often the enemies of peace today. Some promote a sense of community—and not just within our cosy churches. Some get to know neighbours and colleagues, and allow themselves to be known in return.

Most of us avoid aggression, swearing, bullying, violence. I do, I run a mile! Chicken, that's me, or else ostrich. Neither looks anything like the peace-making child of God, yet God's children have been given a ministry of reconciliation between God and humankind (2 Corinthians 5:11–21). A teenager told me how she'd come back from buying an ice-cream in a seaside resort to find a man shouting at her two friends. Apparently he'd asked if they were Christians and when they said no, he kept yelling that they'd go to hell. Another teenager commented how different that sounded from Christians he'd met. They stand every Saturday night outside a nightclub at closing time, serving free hot chocolate and chatting to people. Not getting at them, he said, but getting to know them. These teenagers aren't Christians, but it was pretty clear which had impressed them, which was more likely to make peace and, in the end, reconcile them to God.

I wouldn't want to stand outside a grotty bar in the cold, late at night, chatting to drunken kids with attitude. You're vulnerable, being that kind of peacemaker, and it wouldn't feel very peaceful: there are fights most weekends. Yet Jesus sent out his disciples as sheep among wolves (Matthew 10:16). He himself came to make peace as a child, as a vulnerable baby. As a man he mixed with the less respectable members of society because 'it's the sick who need a doctor'. The Prince of Peace, he allowed himself to be crucified in order to reconcile humankind with God. In what ways does he want us to make peace in this new year?

As I write, Chris Patten is currently the European Commissioner for External Affairs. Before that, he was the last Governor of Hong Kong. In 1999 he chaired the Independent Committee which reported on the future of policing in Northern Ireland. He writes:

Peacemaking involves, above all, a generosity of spirit which is difficult enough to show in our personal lives and is even more of a problem when it becomes tangled with political issues. You have to remember the past—as the Old Testament reminds us—the better to forget it.

For me, the most moving parable in the Gospels is the story of the prodigal son. This should perhaps be required reading for anyone trying to end a bitter dispute.

Let us pray for ourselves and for all peacemakers, echoing the words of Zechariah the father of John the Baptist, that, 'By the tender mercy of our God, the dawn from on high will break upon us, to give light to those who sit in darkness and in the shadow of death, to guide our feet into the way of peace.'

Tradition or risk?

Introduction

Every time a car passed she tried to chuck herself under it. Seventeen at the most, she'd just bust up with her boyfriend. I was on front gate duty on Boxing Night, trying to calm her down, keeping her warm with blankets and tea. After nearly an hour we persuaded her to go back inside. Shortly afterwards she took an overdose. An ambulance whisked her away to hospital. No, we don't know what happened—that's normal.

For eleven years, Cathy Day and her husband Nigel have served as volunteers on the night shift of the charity 'Crisis'. One morning they tried to wake a guest, only to find that he had died in the night, but normally they'll be mopping up vomit, dealing with epileptic fits or trouble-shooting problems concerning drugs or mental health, which are on the increase. 'We're given some information but you have to fly by the seat of your pants, really,' Cathy explained. The rest of the year she works for the Police Complaints Authority. Nigel is part-time church leader and part-time consultant manager to a golf wholesale business. So why do they spend seven nights of the festive season in some London warehouse, doing difficult and unpleasant things for strangers?

It started because we'd grown dissatisfied with the whole overindulgence of Christmas. But now we've met the people, we're there for a more positive reason—it's where Jesus would be.

So does 'Crisis' really help these people?

It depends on which level. Some people are there year after year, which is great because it means they haven't died, but they've not got sorted either. Many other guests are vulnerably housed rather than street-homeless. Lonely and isolated, they use the services, meet people and have a good time. Occasionally we see really positive outcomes. One guy arrived with his face badly beaten and his hair matted. After a shower and a haircut, he stopped drinking, began talking coherently and spent all week in Arts and Crafts. When he left, he gave the volunteers the Christmas cards that he'd made, to thank them for giving him a new start.

Another lad had run away from home two years previously. 'Wouldn't you like to be in touch?' a volunteer asked him. No, his family would never accept him, after all he'd done. After talking further, he gave her permission to phone his home. It was Christmas morning. The family couldn't believe it. 'We've been so worried. Of course he can come back!' One of the volunteers drove him over there and they were reconciled, on Christmas Day.

The power of the Christmas story does not reside in the cosy self-sufficiency of our traditions but in the vulnerability of the shepherds, the foreign sages and the young couple far from home who all dared to associate with a baby in a manger... and who became part of history.

24 December

In those days a decree went out from Emperor Augustus that all the world should be registered. This was the first registration and was taken while Quirinius was governor of Syria. All went to their own towns to be registered. Joseph also went from the town of Nazareth in Galilee to Judea, to the city of David called Bethlehem, because he was descended from the house and family of David. He went to be registered with Mary, to whom he was engaged and who was expecting a child. While they were there, the time came for her to deliver her child. And she gave birth to her firstborn son and wrapped him in bands of cloth, and laid him in a manger, because there was no place for them in the inn.

LUKE 2:1–7

The words of this passage may be so familiar, so much a part of our Christmas tradition, that we don't really hear them any more. I pulled myself up short when I went looking for the donkey—the one poor Mary had to ride all that way from Nazareth. Despite starring in the 'Little Donkey' song and featuring in thousands of nativity plays each year, it doesn't exist—not in Matthew and not in Luke. Neither Mark nor John feature the story of Jesus' birth in Bethlehem at all. Perhaps some artist, long ago, decided that a heavily pregnant Mary couldn't have walked so far. Ambulances with blue flashing lights hadn't been invented, so he chose a mode of transport possibly available to a poor woman of the time—the famous 'Little Donkey'. But, with or without this animal, travelling long distances isn't great for a heavily pregnant woman, especially when she can't phone ahead to secure a bed for the night.

I spent Christmas in hospital one year, having given birth to my first baby on 23 December. There I was in a safe, clean ward, with trolleys and lifts, painkillers, sterile dressings and skilled staff to check everything, yet still it felt scary. I was 27, had read the books, seen the video, attended all the ante-natal classes and practised my breathing exercises. Mary, possibly as young as 14, may have had little idea of what to expect.

During Christmas Eve they dimmed the lights for a few minutes on the maternity ward. In one of those moments I'll never forget, caped nurses with lanterns walked down the corridor softly singing, 'Away in a manger'. Looking in wonder at my day-old son—who had a very special crib for a bed, with a mattress and blankets, a supply of nappies and even red ribbons for Christmas time—I couldn't get over the risk, the pain and uncertainty, the anything-but-cosy circumstances surrounding the birth of the Son of God.

Even in a modern hospital, all is not plain sailing. I talked to Margaret Easton, a staff nurse who works nights in a special-care baby unit, and asked her what it was like there.

It's quiet and hot, the lights are dim and the monitoring machines beep. Sometimes that indicates that something is wrong with a baby, which can be very disconcerting to a nurse who is new to the unit, or indeed to the parents of the babies. The unit's very technical and, unlike most other wards, we have no verbal communication with the patients.

Doesn't it worry you?

Yes, sometimes. Nowadays babies are viable at 24 weeks gestation, and can weigh as little as 500 grams—which is like half a bag of sugar! New drugs are amazing, but their exact dosage, and that of oxygen, has to be so carefully worked out. We double-check with another nurse, each using a different calculator. Ten years or so ago, though, many of these babies would not have survived. It's very satisfying when you see them going home and then see photos of healthy, happy children two or four years on.

What happens in the unit over the Christmas period?

If parents with a baby in the unit have other children at home, they feel very torn. They cannot spend as much time as they would like at home with their family. Though siblings are allowed in the unit, obviously it's not the same. For staff on nights, work continues very much as usual, except that on Christmas Eve the sister of the unit, dressed as Father Christmas, puts a filled stocking on each of the cots or incubators.

You're a mum yourself—how does your work affect your family this time of year?

It certainly disrupts our family Christmases! Some years we'll go to my mum's but may have to be back in time for my night duty. This year I'm working Christmas Eve and Boxing Night, so I'll prepare the meal before I go to sleep on Christmas morning and my husband will cook the vegetables, etc, and dish up. I'll get up earlier than usual and we'll open presents in the afternoon. Our children used to find it hard to wait when they were younger.

How does your faith help you at work?

Other nurses ask, 'If there's a God of love, why does he let babies suffer so?' What can you say? It's not easy. I find it hard when I see young babies die. I would find it even harder if I had no faith. We all have to die at some time and I believe God is sovereign, so I can only leave matters like that in his hands.

What about the parents?

Being on nights, I don't see the parents that much. It's often very difficult for them—having a baby leaves you feeling vulnerable and emotional at the best of times. They've been expecting to go home with a healthy little one but now maybe their baby is undergoing unpleasant procedures or attached to bleeping machines. Some parents are in denial at this time and can turn on the doctors and nurses. Others ask, 'Why didn't God stop this happening?' or 'What have we done to deserve this?' I'd like to work days sometimes, so I could listen to them and be there for them. Perhaps then I could offer them a little more help.

Lord God, we're all vulnerable. Life from the very beginning is a risk. Help us to see that you hold each of our lives in your hands. And help us to see past the traditions we've built around Christmas to the fact that you risked sending your Son to be born into this world, not even into the relative safety of a modern maternity ward but into an occupied country. Knowing that you understand, we pray for all parents today who feel for their children's vulnerability, especially the parents of tiny babies. We pray for the doctors, nurses and everyone who works over the Christmas and New Year period in order to make the world safer for us. We thank you for them and we lift up their families to you, too.

Christmas Day

How beautiful upon the mountains are the feet of the messenger who announces peace, who brings good news, who announces salvation, who says to Zion, 'Your God reigns.' Listen! Your sentinels lift up their voices, together they sing for joy; for in plain sight they see the return of the Lord to Zion. Break forth together into singing, you ruins of Jerusalem; for the Lord has comforted his people, he has redeemed Jerusalem. The Lord has bared his holy arm before the eyes of all the nations; and all the ends of the earth shall see the salvation of our God.

ISAIAH 52:7–10

The preacher's joking reference right at the start of his sermon on Christmas morning proved a bad idea. 'Don't worry about whether you've set your ovens correctly!' All over the church for the next ten minutes, women could be seen fidgeting and glancing at their watches. I can get myself in such a state preparing a non-festive meal for a couple of guests that I snap everyone's head off. Focusing on God in worship on Christmas morning takes a major effort of will!

Just as well, then, that Christmas, the coming of the Messiah, is not about perfection but about redemption. That's not a bad thing to remember if the mince pies have gone soggy, everyone has the flu, the burst boiler can't be repaired until 27 January and you just know that cousin Flossie, who arrived to stay yesterday, is going to upset everyone again. If everything's wonderful, praise God and enjoy your Christmas! But if you are feeling like the 'ruins of Jerusalem' this morning, it's still OK to let rip and have a good sing. Jesus is not bringing condemnation but good news, salvation, peace. This is the gospel. The messenger (or angel) brings good news to those whose lives are in a mess—for example, to Israel who had messed up their relationship with God, done everything wrong and ended up in exile in a pagan, hostile land. Good news—new beginnings are possible because our God reigns!

Veronica Heley, a freelance writer of over 40 books, thought she had bitten off more than she could chew when it came to 'Lighting the Lane':

The traders were discussing how to entertain upwards of 2,000 people on the evening they light up the trees in our local parade for Christmas. Most shops stay open with stalls outside, and entertainment is laid on. How to make this bigger and better for the Millennium?

I said, 'How about a nativity pageant?' It's a wonderful opportunity to remind people of the real meaning of Christmas. Our local schools are so multi-cultural that Christianity has been sidelined.

That's where I began to climb mountains, for the producer dropped out, Mary declined the honour, wise men fell sick, the costumes were too short, and general apathy ruled. Doggedly I wrote the text and persuaded the choir to take part. I begged lanterns, made and ironed costumes, found another Mary and more wise men... and then there were technical problems with the sound. On the plus side, the angel wore his own very splendid Kenyan robes, and an 80-year-old shepherd grew a beard. We ended up with a mix of adults and children; I'd have liked to have added animals, too.

Problems remained right up to the last minute. One day I was praying in church and fighting off depression. Opening the Bible, this bit from Isaiah came up: 'How wonderful it is to see a messenger coming across the mountains bringing good news, the news of peace.'

We did take the good news to the people. There were 5,000 people at the event on the night, and as the pageant was staged one woman was overheard saying to her child, 'Look! This is what it is all about!'

Lord, help us to see once more what it's all about today—and to sing!

26 December

Let the same mind be in you that was in Christ Jesus, who, though he was in the form of God, did not regard equality with God as something to be exploited, but emptied himself, taking the form of a slave, being born in human likeness... he humbled himself and became obedient to the point of death— even death on a cross. Therefore God also highly exalted him and gave him the name that is above every name, so that at the name of Jesus every knee should bend, in heaven and on earth and under the earth, and every tongue should confess that Jesus Christ is Lord, to the glory of God the Father.

PHILIPPIANS 2:5–11

This is not the Prologue to John's Gospel, but it has the same ring of wonder and earth-shattering significance. Since before time began, God's Son knew adoration, creativity, joy, power, knowledge, wisdom and beauty as he enjoyed fellowship with the Godhead and heavenly beings. And now the unthinkable. He 'empties himself'. Master of all becomes a slave. What pain! If I emptied myself of family, friends and church, of writing, books, house, car and garden, of telephone and television, of freedom, achievements, education and knowledge... it would be easier to face death, which the Prince of Life endured too. Nothing was more important to him than bringing a fallen people back into a right relationship with the Godhead. There were no guarantees, yet he took the risk, leaving behind his birthright, his 'traditions'. We are told to have the same mind that was in Christ Jesus. The first stage is to empty ourselves.

I don't know about you but around Christmas time I'm normally running on what Railtrack might call 'the wrong kind of emptiness'— more likely to bawl out the family and kick the rabbit than to 'have the same mind that was in Christ Jesus'. Yet serving others is exactly what Jesus did on earth. The key seems to be that he remained obedient. Because of that, God 'highly exalted him'. Makes you want to worship him, doesn't it? To shout that every knee should bend and every tongue confess that he is Lord, to the glory of God the Father! To pray he'll help us to 'be blameless and innocent, children of God without blemish in the midst of a crooked and perverse generation, in which [we] shine like stars in the world'. For that is what the passage goes on to say (v. 15). We are called to be different, to take risks and, like stars, as the dark and cold around us increases, to shine ever more brightly.

Audrey Evans from County Wicklow is someone who gives of herself. Here she writes about her exhausting but enjoyable Christmases!

Someone once said, 'If you want something done, ask the busiest person that you know and they will find time to do it.' That is probably a good description of me. I have a husband, four children and a large extended family so I am always busy cooking and entertaining. For many years I have been involved with the Girls' Brigade, the Leprosy Mission, the Healer Prayer Movement and Scripture Union. I also work part-time for a house-minding agency. We have dogs, cats, ducks and an aviary of tropical birds all demanding attention.

Christmas is such a busy time in our home. On Christmas Eve our extended family converge on my mother's apartment to celebrate her birthday. Next morning I rise early to check that the oven has started to cook our very large turkey. We all then attend the morning service in our local church. As soon as it ends, crowds of people rush to the beach where the annual Christmas Day swim takes place. There is a great air of festivity as people arrive, some in fancy costume, some sponsored by companies who want to raise money for charity. Only the insane take the plunge, as the sea water in Greystones is always freezing. Photographers are there from local newspapers to record the annual event. I have taken part in this lunacy on several occasions with my dogs swimming along beside me! We usually invite a few friends home for a drink (a hot one for me) and some finger-food.

If the turkey is cooked on time, we should be tucking into our Christmas dinner at about 3.00 pm. When we have had more than enough to eat, we adjourn to the lounge where we exchange our gifts. Once that event is completed, anything can happen. Some folk fall asleep, others play silly games, while the younger members of the family disappear into another room to watch the television. Sometimes we sit around the piano and sing carols. I usually fall into bed totally exhausted on Christmas night.

Next day is my day: breakfast in bed, no housework, I am waited on hand and foot. Would you believe that Boxing Day is my birthday!

Lord, as we give of ourselves, you give us so much—the beauty of the world around us, the riches we find in the companionship of others, food and laughter, creativity and variety, and your love!

27 December

A Samaritan woman came to draw water, and Jesus said to
her, 'Give me a drink.' (His disciples had gone to the city to
buy food.) The Samaritan woman said to him, 'How is it that
you, a Jew, ask a drink of me, a woman of Samaria?' (Jews do
not share things in common with Samaritans.) Jesus answered
her, 'If you knew the gift of God, and who it is that is saying
to you, "Give me a drink," you would have asked him, and he
would have given you living water.'

JOHN 4:7–10

In the stunningly beautiful Burne-Jones window depicting this scene
in St Peter's Church, London, Jesus looks too weak-wristed to haul
water out of a well. I don't think that rings true. Nevertheless, he let
himself be vulnerable. When he saw people who needed liberating,
he'd not approach them like the general of a liberating army, wearing
full armour—for however benevolent the army, that would scare them
off. He didn't bash people with the gospel but gently asked the
woman for help and won her over that way.

No wonder the disciples were 'astonished' when they returned. At
the very well where their forefather Jacob had watered Rachel's sheep
and fallen in love with her, they found Jesus chatting to a loose
woman. He'd put himself in her debt by asking for a drink of water—
he a Jew and she one of those sad Samaritans who had gone astray and
been abandoned by God! Rabbis weren't supposed to speak to any
woman alone. Spiritual development for females was supposed to take
place at home, if at all. Women's testimony was not allowed in a court
of law. Jesus had not only been seemingly unwise but had broken
almost every taboo the disciples could think of.

Too embarrassed to ask him why, the disciples took refuge in the details of everyday life. Had he eaten? Jesus replied, 'My food is to do the will of him who sent me and to complete his work', and then started talking about bringing in the harvest (vv. 34–38). They must have thought he was mad, talking of harvest, when surely he'd blown his ministry! No one in that place, Jew or Samaritan, would follow him now. And yet, as the woman told the story to her fellow townspeople, they believed in Jesus. They invited him to stay and many followed him. Afterwards, even the Galileans who had tried to throw him off a cliff welcomed him because they had seen the things that he had done.

Jesus refused to be boxed in by respectability, religious tradition, mindsets, gender stereotypes, prejudice or fear. He would reach out to any person, if he knew that his Father wanted him to. He bothered with the despised Samaritan woman; his conversation with her is one of the longest recorded anywhere in the Bible. He risks reaching out to us today—holding out the precious gift of life in all its fullness, enabling us to worship in spirit and in truth.

Anne Atkins, novelist, columnist and broadcaster, lives with her husband and four children in Fulham, London. I asked what she thought about risk.

I suppose the biggest risk many of us take is marriage, especially if we believe in Christian marriage and the old promises to share all our worldly goods, to love, honour and obey. In marriage you give yourself away and so lay yourself open to abuse. Before we were engaged, Shaun's sister said to him, 'I don't understand your attitude. You'd do anything for Anne.' Well, yes—that's what a committed relationship is all about.

But what happens if we don't take risks? This is a materialistic example, but about two and a half years ago we saw a house which would have been perfect for us. It cost far more than we could afford and friends warned, 'You'd be taking a terrible risk. Suppose you lost your jobs or the bottom fell out of the housing market—you'd be wiped out.' So we stayed put. None of the things we feared have happened and now we regret our decision. We could have owned a lovely home for the family if only we'd had the courage to risk it. There's a price to pay for not taking risks.

In this passage, not only does Jesus risk a huge amount but the woman does too. Supposing she'd not risked believing him!

What risks are you asking me to take today, Lord, especially in the area of reaching out to other human beings? Where have I been inflexible in my relationships, hiding behind convention, habit or judgmental prejudice? How can I give myself to others more fully—the way Jesus gave himself for me?

28 December

As he walked by the Sea of Galilee, he saw two brothers,
Simon, who is called Peter, and Andrew his brother, casting a
net into the sea—for they were fishermen. And he said to
them, 'Follow me, and I will make you fish for people.'
Immediately they left their nets and followed him. As he went
from there, he saw two other brothers, James son of Zebedee
and his brother John, in the boat with their father, Zebedee,
mending their nets, and he called them. Immediately they left
the boat and their father, and followed him.

MATTHEW 4:18–22

I find this story hard to believe. Beforehand Matthew tells us only that
Jesus leaves Nazareth, makes his home in Capernaum and proclaims,
'Repent, for the kingdom of heaven has come near.' Why would four
fishermen immediately leave their livelihood to trail after some manic
street preacher?

What could have influenced them? His hypnotic eyes? These were
toughies supporting their families by hauling in great catches of fish
and maybe gutting them too. Nicknamed 'Sons of Thunder', James
and John were successful business partners of Andrew and Simon
(Mark mentions hired men as well as their father in their boat).
Fishermen who face the unpredictable dangers of storms in tiny boats
to earn their living may be superstitious, but they also love tradition
and stick with the familiar—especially their boats. They don't chase
after Pied Piper strangers who shout strange warnings and make fancy
promises—and nor should we!

But Luke starts the story much earlier, telling us how, after rejection
in his home town of Nazareth, Jesus stayed in the lakeside town of
Capernaum, teaching in its synagogue every Sabbath, astounding the

people because he spoke—and cast out demons—with authority. Word spread around the region. When Jesus visited Simon's house and rid his mother-in-law of a high fever, sick and demon-possessed people clamoured for attention. Having spent all night healing or delivering them, at dawn Jesus tried to escape the crowds. They begged him to stay but he told them he must proclaim the good news in other cities.

Then, after telling them where to catch the biggest netful ever, Jesus asked just four men to follow him and catch people. Now we can understand and believe the story—given half a chance, most of the town would have followed him too!

Jesus still asks us to take risks. He may ask us to change our lifestyle or our livelihood, even to go to prison or to die for him, but not before we've seen what he's like, not before we know him, not before he's shown us his heart, his vision, his power and his goodness. He used, but also subverted, tradition—speaking with compelling authority in the synagogues, leaving his home town, his family, the trade he'd learnt, to do the work to which God had called him. Like the best leaders, he was asking no more of his followers than he was prepared to do himself.

So what's most important to us—the great traditions of Christmas, Advent, New Year, church, culture and family… or following Jesus? The message of his story puts risk way above tradition—and it isn't very comfortable!

Dave Whitman grew up in an English village but now leads a team from Agapé (formerly Campus Crusade for Christ) at the scientific university of Novosibirsk, a large town in the middle of Siberia. He and his Russian wife have two young children. He writes:

Although being a fisherman is not the safest of jobs, it is the kind of profession that is familiar—you grow up with it, as the skills are handed down from your grandfather and father. Being a missionary in Russia is usually not dangerous, but it is certainly not familiar.

Up until this year our small church met in a school, so we were never able to celebrate Christmas on the 25th as it is a normal working day. It can be unsettling when, for those around you, it is just another snowy Monday. You feel like telling them all to wake up, or shouting, 'Don't you know something special is happening?' Maybe the fishermen felt that way as they left all that was familiar to follow Jesus; they sensed what others did not, that he was something special.

Just this week, a friend and colleague was very nearly killed by two young men who had asked her to 'tell them about God'—an invitation no missionary could refuse. Doing our job demands that we are vulnerable. There are no certainties when you follow an itinerant Messiah. He alone is your guarantee. We live knowing that the government could split our family up, with doctors we cannot fully trust and with a thousand other uncertainties. This world of hidden threats could be overwhelming if he was not with us just as much as he was with those fishermen.

I like the traditions of Christmas, but maybe our church with no place to celebrate is closer to the reality of overcrowded Bethlehem—and maybe our life of everyday risks is closer to those young parents, far away from home with their fragile newborn baby.

Pray for those in risky situations, then ask what risks God is asking you to take.

29 December

Peter got out of the boat, started walking on the water, and came toward Jesus. But when he noticed the strong wind, he became frightened, and beginning to sink, he cried out, 'Lord, save me!' Jesus immediately reached out his hand and caught him, saying to him, 'You of little faith, why did you doubt?'
MATTHEW 14:29–31

It had been a long, stormy night in the small fishing vessel, far from land. It's understandable that the sleepless disciples thought a ghost was walking towards them in the half-light of dawn. Yet Peter heard Jesus' voice and went to him! He didn't have to leap out of that boat that stormy night. He wasn't following an established tradition of water-walking. It was pure risk—or pure faith! Jesus' other friends all stayed put, but Peter was staking his life on this being his Lord. At the time of leaping, he knew Jesus wouldn't let him down, but away from the limited shelter afforded by the boat, Peter felt the full force of the wind. Panic overcame trust, fear won over faith and he began to sink. I'd have done exactly the same, except that I'd never have dared to leap, or even to go out in the boat in the first place! I'd have been tucked up in a nice warm bed back home, catching up on some sleep before another ordinary day. Yet Jesus set out to create more surprises than traditions! He'll ask few of us to walk on water, but he does challenge us to step out of our 'boats' and follow his ways, not ours.

While I was writing this, a friend phoned. A couple of months beforehand, she'd embarked on some brand new challenges, stepping out of her rut, her comfort zones. After weeks of having to travel long distances and meet deadlines, she'd arrived home almost sick with tiredness, only to find that her 15-year-old son had been rushed from school to hospital with a severe asthma attack. Her husband's work had taken him to the other end of the country for a few days and no one else could bring her now-recovered son home again. After doing so herself, my friend retired to bed with her migraine.

'It makes me want to give up, to stay at home and simply be a mum,' she said. 'Then I'd be there for emergencies and we wouldn't all have this hassle. But then emergencies only seem to happen when I launch out and do something which I believe God is asking of me.'

Anything new can feel as stressful as walking on the water at times when we don't know what is expected of us or what is likely to happen, when we don't know how we or our family will react when additional pressures come. My friend said, 'I could have coped, Chris, if my hormones hadn't chosen that moment to peak!' When everything seems to conspire against us, if we are to overcome, the only course of action is to listen to what Jesus is saying to us and to obey. He may not, as with Peter, lift us out of the water, return us to the boat and then still the storm. He may reach out his hand in order to help us walk and then run with him over the gigantic waves, to win the race and to gain the prize of our high calling.

The further we leap into God's upside-down kingdom, the more things are likely to be upset. But if we stay in the boat or, worse, on the familiar dry land, we'll never know his real power.

Lance Pierson is a performer of poetry and one-man shows, both for churches and for secular audiences. He writes:

It was December 1975. Some businessmen asked me to talk about Christmas at their monthly lunch club. And I was stuck.

I could think of nothing to say that others hadn't already said much better. Ah! If others had already said it, perhaps I could read their words and bring them back to life... Not daring to ask permission, I simply took the plunge: instead of my thoughts, the businessmen got a mix of Dickens and Milton and Peanuts cartoons!

That lunch launched me on a new career. No longer a speaker, but a performer of other people's writing. I still do a Christmas show each year, but now others as well, all year long.

The big step forward came in 1986. I decided to offer a re-enactment of 90 minutes of the Acts of the Apostles. I couldn't simply read this; I had to learn it by heart. It's as many words as a star part in Shakespeare. I gulped... was I being too ambitious? But there was no going back: the date was fixed, the audience came, I prayed, 'Lord, save me!' and he made sure I didn't sink.

Show me where I need to step out of my comfort zones for you, Lord.

30 December

'Blessed are those who are persecuted for righteousness' sake, for theirs is the kingdom of heaven. Blessed are you when people revile you and persecute you and utter all kinds of evil against you falsely on my account. Rejoice and be glad, for your reward is great in heaven, for in the same way they persecuted the prophets who were before you.'

MATTHEW 5:10–12

This is not the kind of Christmas message we want to hear, yet it resonates with the most difficult and unpopular part of the Christmas story, so Jesus earned the right to say it, if anyone did. Even before he was old enough to make any conscious decision, Jesus was persecuted for righteousness' sake—hidden, not like Moses in the bulrushes, but in Egypt none the less, a country that signified slavery and oppression to the Jews. The Jewish ruler, King Herod, should have known better but, just like Pharaoh, he was prepared to wipe out a generation of children when he thought he saw a threat to his own power. The people needed a saviour again—only this time Jesus would rescue them not from the corruption of a cruel ruler, but from the effects of evil on their lives.

In many countries, the risks involved in following Jesus are all too real, whether they involve lost opportunities for work and education, or losing friends and family, liberty and even life itself. In the UK, people might think us strange for going to church. Some ignore us, others may tease us, but they are not allowed to kill all our children!

Self-preservation is still a powerful instinct, though. How would we react if someone in the same train carriage was attacked? Or if we were in the position to expose dangerous or corrupt practices in our workplace? If a roomful of people were blaspheming and rubbishing

Jesus, would we be prepared to bring the opposite spirit to bear? This is where I get really uncomfortable, for instead of praying, 'Jesus, what would you want me to do?' then taking the risk of obeying him, I'm more likely to hide behind tradition or excuses. Tradition says, 'British people mind their own business.' Excuses might be, 'I'm only a poor weak female and can't change this' or, 'If I get involved and get hurt, what about my children?' (Of course, I'm not at all worried about me, oh no!)

So, unlike Jesus, I don't have a right to comment. I'm not even sure what the answer is, except that, especially when my children were young, I would have taken any risk to protect them from attack. My natural human instinct, allied to my love for them, made me strong and brave and determined enough for anything. So, it's a dangerous prayer, but: *'Lord, help me to love you with all my heart and mind and soul and strength and to love my neighbour as myself!'*

Pam MacKenzie develops education and literacy programmes in developing countries. For six years she has worked with Paul Raj, an Indian evangelist working among tribal peoples in Andhra Pradesh. Over 30 years he has built up churches totalling 45,000 baptized adults, and supports over 13 schools with accompanying hostels, vocational schools and an engineering college. On Pam's most recent visit, everything seemed to be coming against Paul and his work. She writes of one crisis after another:

When I arrived, Paul's life was already under threat from Muslims who objected that some of their number had become Christians. Then floods made 100,000 homeless, including 10,000 from the churches. They had nothing to eat, and no donor organization would help, so Paul took out a massive bank loan and bought food for them himself. Then rumours spread that a girl had been raped and murdered at the engineering college—yet no girls were missing! Many local churches had already been bombed by Hindu militants, and several priests, mainly Roman Catholics, murdered. Then a Lutheran bishop from nearby was hacked to death by three men one afternoon. As Chairman of the Andhra Pradesh Council of Churches, Paul attended his funeral and questioned the police. Paul is known for his fearless stand for truth. The next day an anonymous phone call said he would meet a fate like the bishop's if he investigated further and two letters threatened to bomb his churches. He told me this almost casually.

Paul's trust in the Lord inspires confidence and so I said I would stand next to him during the church service... You can't afford to let fear grip you or you'd never do anything. Although we all felt that it was not yet Paul's time to die, he simply takes each day, each hour at a time. 'If I go, I go to the Lord!' he says and he keeps refusing a police guard, saying, 'What would that say about my God?' We trust that God will look after him—and all of us. Paul feels that the persecution will be good for the church in India—it will refine it; and it will make the church rely not on buildings but on a relationship with Jesus. It won't stop them growing!

Pray for anyone you know of who is suffering persecution.

SIX

Go on giving—
or shop till you drop?

Introduction

As the old year passes, the early days of January focus on materialism —on the sales, the Christmas bills arriving, and on our return to work. Yet we're approaching Epiphany, that moment when the eternal breaks in to transform the mundane.

Epiphany is also when we think about the gifts of the Magi, and giving is costly. I talked to Sarah Clunton, a dedicated junior school teacher. For 16 years, she has given well beyond the call of duty in terms of time, energy, prayer, herself... Knowing how much she cares, I asked what happens when she reaches the point of exhaustion.

When I feel that I'm getting nowhere at all, often I call in friends to stand alongside and pray with me. In a sense, anyone could teach children who want to learn, but I also long to help the ones who fail and whose lives are in a mess. Though I believe I'm sowing seeds at school, I have to face the fact that I may never see much growth, let alone fruit—and that's hard.

The other year, four real troublemakers in my class shook me. Never before have children gone on refusing to accept my discipline, but these would run out of lessons and get into all sorts of trouble. Yet they were so lovable. A friend and I prayed regularly for one girl from a difficult background who influenced the others greatly. Good and bad were locked inside her—anger, resentment, but also creativity. We prayed that she would open up like a shell. We saw little progress, though maybe things would have been even worse had we not prayed. One day we felt we were achieving nothing. Our prayers were just words. All we could do was to cry out, 'Oh God, oh God!' or, for variety, 'God, oh!'

We did see the girl's behaviour quieten in class, which helped the atmosphere greatly. But she continued to cause problems in the playground and had serious run-ins with the head teacher. She left our school still on a rocky road—so this isn't a good story for your book, is it?

I disagree. Our human thinking would prefer the whole class to have repented, met Jesus, found healing for damage in their lives, gained their PhDs by the age of 15 and spent the rest of their lives extending the kingdom of God across the world. If God is God, dramatic miracles can happen, but more often they don't. I found myself thinking of that great passage about people of faith, Hebrews 11. Alongside the likes of Abraham and Moses, it commends the faith of unknowns who apparently achieved very little. The eternal results are God's responsibility and only he sees the whole from a true perspective. The giving is up to us—and he thinks it worth recording.

31 December

Ho, everyone who thirsts, come to the waters; and you that have no money, come, buy and eat! Come, buy wine and milk without money and without price. Why do you spend your money for that which is not bread, and your labour for that which does not satisfy? Listen carefully to me, and eat what is good, and delight yourselves in rich food. Incline your ear, and come to me; listen, so that you may live.

ISAIAH 55:1–3

Most thirsty people on New Year's Eve end up the next day with a sore head and an empty pocket, plus some regrets. Others thirst not just for alcohol and a 'good time' but for a new start. However, no magic wand is waved at midnight on 31 December. If we remember our fine New Year's resolutions at all after a fortnight, we may feel 'hungover', with our heads sore from efforts to 'do better' and plenty of regrets.

Isaiah suggests that, before we can give, or change, we need to receive God's grace and goodness—even to feast upon them. Instead of shopping (or drinking) till we drop, we can sit back and receive life itself in all its fullness—riches without price. Far better than material riches like dishwashers, computers or new cars, riches like relationships, truth or being God's friend will last for eternity.

It's a timely message as people think about returning to work after the Christmas break. Longer and longer hours, traffic jams and crowded trains, stress levels increasing year on year—yet wasn't technology supposed to free us for the things that matter? The inventions that should save time, the faxes and e-mails, often lead to a 'last minute rush' mentality. Increasingly, people feel driven. Even for those with less stressful lives, all the food and parties and shopping in the world will satisfy us for only a short time, while Jesus will satisfy us for eternity!

Those words may be true, but how do they work out in practice in the world in which we live?

Irene Williams works with adults who have learning disabilities, helping them to develop communication and life skills. She told me about how God challenged her attitude to the Christmas period. I've included her words near the end of this book, rather than at the beginning, because she said it took a whole year of prayer for her to change. God rarely 'zaps' us overnight, especially when it's a case of altering our mindset radically from the norm, but as we listen to and cooperate with him, his slowly transforming grace brings all kinds of benefits and opportunities. Irene writes:

Christmas proved a yearly challenge to me as a Christian. Was it going to mean joy or hassle? I knew it was a time to reflect on the love of God through his gift to us of his Son, Jesus. I knew it was a time to celebrate his gifts of joy and peace with family and friends. But with good food to prepare and eat, gifts to give and receive, cards to write, shopping to do, people to visit, more cards to write, yet more shopping… it often proved impossible to keep everything in perspective, to find time to enjoy God's peace and joy and to appreciate this Christmas season. Pressures increased as the days sped by. October—only ten weeks to go—so much to do and plan and buy. So tempting to join in the cry of, 'I'll be glad when it's all over, won't you?'

Gently, but persistently, the Lord challenged me. Christ had to be the focus—and in particular, at this time of year, his joy and peace. But how? Prayer and his grace, asking the Holy Spirit for guidance, making time to listen, all played their part, and then a talk by Fiona Castle confirmed that a radical change was possible.

Now I set aside time early on to shop and start writing cards earlier too. I plan meals and buy food as far in advance as possible. I allocate time for visiting elderly and housebound friends so that my normal visits aren't squeezed out in a pre-Christmas rush. After Christmas we go to stay in the country with my husband's mother and enjoy God's creation on long walks. That way, although lots of people stay with us over Christmas and the catering can be tiring, I return to work refreshed in the New Year.

I haven't 'arrived'. I'm sure I'll feel pressured again. But my prayer for myself and for every one of us is that we'll take time to meditate on all that Christ is for us—to enjoy the best gift of all. I pray that we'll resist the temptation to join in the pre-Christmas grumbling and instead share something of the Lord's peace and love with those around.

Father God, thank you that you loved the world so much that you gave your only Son, so that everyone who believes in him may not perish but may have eternal life.

New Year's Day

Seek the Lord while he may be found, call upon him while he
is near; let the wicked forsake their way, and the unrighteous
their thoughts; let them return to the Lord, that he may have
mercy on them, and to our God, for he will abundantly pardon.
For my thoughts are not your thoughts, nor are your ways my
ways, says the Lord. For as the heavens are higher than the
earth, so are my ways higher than your ways and my thoughts
than your thoughts.

ISAIAH 55:6–9

The New Year is a time when we think about new beginnings and a
clean start. All of us have histories, made up of good and bad, right
and wrong—of things which help and things which hinder us. As we
look back over the past year, it's all too easy to wallow in the mistakes
we've made, again (will we never learn?). We've fallen for the same
temptations, hurting people that we love in the process. We've failed
to do all kinds of things that God has asked of us. We are miserable
offenders and there is no health in us—but that's not the whole story!

I've caught myself thinking that, having been a Christian for
many years, I should have matured into something like fine, vintage
champagne which will gladden the heart of God. Clearly something's
gone wrong. I've been 'corked', letting putrefying bacteria in and
leaving only a horrid taste in the mouth. It's no good calling on
God—he's holy; he wouldn't want to be around someone like me. It's
therefore no good taking comfort from the passage above. He is not
near and, even if he were, what utter cheek for me to repent yet again!
As to the possibility of my giving anything good to God or to people,
forget it—anything I would give would make them sick to the
stomach.

That's an extreme way of putting it, but we all feel at some point that our sin, shame, guilt and regret separate us from God. What rubbish! His ways are higher than our ways, his thoughts than our thoughts. It's almost impossible for us to understand why he should bother with, let alone love humankind, after all the grief we've given him. But it remains a fact that Jesus chose to spend most of his time with sinners, not saints—and the miracle of the cross means that a holy God is able to come near to us, however vile we feel. Like the Father in Jesus' story of the lost son, he doesn't grudgingly 'let us off this time': when we 'return to the Lord' he pardons abundantly—he throws a party!

If we agree with him that our ways and thoughts have been wrong, he's prepared to stick with us as we try to put things right, even when we keep failing. He's not only prepared, but determined, to help us. He knows that we're not much good at keeping New Year (or other) resolutions and that's why he works on our hearts, helping us to change from the inside out. If we cooperate with him, he promises that 'instead of the thorn shall come up the cypress; instead of the brier shall come up the myrtle' (Isaiah 55:13).

Roger Madge's work as a consultant engineer often brings pressure. He told me:

Suppose there's some thought pattern which keeps recurring in your brain— and you decide it's not one you want to be dwelling on. It could be anything from negativity to jealousy, from worry-spirals to inappropriate sexual fantasy. You talk to God about it and he forgives you, but then every time that thought pattern recurs you feel more and more guilty and you try even harder, but you fail again. Well, I'm beginning to see a way through that. I think it's a mixture of self-control and faith—and if the problem's really big it's not that you need superhuman self-control, you just need a bit more faith. It's also vital to recognize the moment when the thought-chain begins because it's then, in the heat of the moment, that you need the presence of mind to take action. That's certainly not the moment to feel guilty. You haven't given in to sin yet and God doesn't remember the sins he's forgiven you in the past. It is a moment to talk to God and say, 'Lord, we've agreed about this. You don't want it and I don't want it—and we've agreed that this is dealt with.' I can honestly say that certain things which have troubled me for years have gone—and in certain cases have not come back!

My God of new beginnings, thank you that your ways are higher than our ways. Thank you that this means you will always love me whatever, *and* that you've provided ways for us to be right—and to stay right—with you and with others.

2 January

From his fullness we have all received, grace upon grace. The law indeed was given through Moses; grace and truth came through Jesus Christ. No one has ever seen God. It is God the only Son, who is close to the Father's heart, who has made him known.

JOHN 1:16–18

They used to call them the January Sales, but these days many sales start on Boxing Day! Instead of present-buying for other people, now we scrabble for ourselves, our homes, our cars, even our computers. Devotees of 'retail therapy' throng to shopping-mall cathedrals. What a difference of spirit in the verses above! They are not about grabbing, not even about our giving, but about God giving freely to us.

We are approaching Epiphany: the root meaning of that word has to do with showing, revealing, making manifest. I walk often on the North Downs near my home. Used to pleasant views over Leatherhead and the woods and fields of the Mole Valley, I could hardly believe it one crisp, pollution-free winter's day. Beyond the small town, I saw the whole of London from the Post Office Tower in the west to Canary Wharf in the east. Spiritually, too, most of us have moments of clear vision, when the eternal breaks through the humdrum of our daily lives and suddenly we see something new of God. Nothing will be quite the same again. The beginning of John's Gospel shines with that kind of vision. Through simple words, God is made manifest—his fullness can never run out. His grace is not limited to certain periods in the year. He gives and gives and gives again.

Most of all, he gives Jesus, who doesn't just tell us about Father God—but makes him known to us. Surely that is worth more than anything we could ever buy! In him, 'steadfast love and faithfulness meet, righteousness and peace kiss each other' (Psalm 85:10). Where grace and truth, love and justice meet, there is God.

If we are to become like him, giving, not grasping, we have to learn first to receive—to love others because he first loved us, to forgive others because he forgave us. If we are ever holy, it is because he reveals his holiness to us. If we experience pure joy, it is because he shares his with us. If we are moved with compassion, it is because he lets us taste his tears. If we keep on giving, it's because that is exactly what he does for us.

Mother and grandmother Mary Reid was until recently a teacher and is now a school governor. She has worked in publishing and edits *Day by Day with God*—Bible reading notes for women, written by women. As a clergy wife, she has had to adapt to living in different places, and as a bishop's wife (she's married to Gavin, formerly Bishop of Maidstone), her life is extremely busy. She enjoys all (or most!) of the entertaining she has to do, probably because she is very much a people-person. She talked about both giving and receiving over the festive season:

God has given so much to us—though all of our experience of Christmas is bound to change over the years and I think you have to separate out the family side from the real, unsentimental part of the Christmas story. When I was teaching, I loved the run-up to Christmas, being able to help five-year-olds sort out Santa from the real nativity story. When my own family were small, we all went along to our parish church on Christmas morning. It was always packed with families from the local community—a very happy occasion. I'm one of those people who prefers singing away in a parish church to choral services in a big cathedral. I miss that and it's strange, too, now our own children are married and maybe spending time with their other halves' families. But on the other hand, now our oldest grandson is 6, it's lovely to see him entering into the whole Christmas story and watching his excitement as he discovers it for himself.

Gavin is incredibly busy the whole year, but from Advent to New Year he never stops. Last year I thought it would be a good idea to have all the family with us on Boxing Day, so we could enjoy an unhurried Christmas lunch together. However, I had forgotten it was Gavin's turn to be at the cathedral for a service that afternoon, so he had to dash off to Canterbury, leaving us to carry on with our 'family Christmas'!

Gavin's office is in our house, so nearly everyone who calls has an appointment. At first I found this very different from our previous home, where friends just dropped by for a cup of tea. That's partly why we bought our first puppy—he was a great ice-breaker and I soon got to know people in our village. It's good to meet people when out walking the dogs (we now have two): there are plenty of lonely and isolated people around, even in a village like ours.

Lord, help us to receive so that we may give.

3 January

'Give, and it will be given to you. A good measure, pressed down, shaken together, running over, will be put into your lap; for the measure you give will be the measure you get back.'
LUKE 6:38

Why is it that every charity you've ever heard of chooses to send out begging letters on the approach to Christmas, just at the time when you're wondering how on earth you're going to buy all those presents? I find myself becoming annoyed and decidedly uncharitable. And now, just as the credit card bills are looming and we're contemplating a hard slog through the dark, cold months before spring arrives, the last thing we need to read is this verse!

God's demands can seem so unreasonable. And yet they fit with the way he created the world. Leafless trees give freely of their blossom after enduring the bare cold of winter. It's snatched away by the wind again—but without the brief, extravagant delight of blossom, no fruit would come.

Some of the happiest people I've met have been those who have very little but still give of themselves without stinting. I'm not too good at that myself. When I give, I usually hold something in reserve, probably because I don't trust God enough. If I give all my time and energy, I might not cope. If we give all our money, well that's absurd, what will we and the family live on?

A friend of mine is bewildered and not a little angry. She lives on virtually nothing herself as she serves development projects in poorer countries. She'll trek through the bush and stay in some primitive village with people who have nothing—and be overwhelmed with the generosity of their hospitality. She's just contacted a local church administrator in England, asking if he knows people who could give accommodation for a few nights to twelve students from a tribal area of India.

'So many?' he replied. 'People here have small houses and big mortgages.' I can see his difficulty. With our houses full of convenience food and labour-saving devices, with our cars and keys and nuclear families, somehow we've lost the ability simply to be 'inconvenienced'—to welcome people into our homes, share with them what we have and maybe entertain angels unawares.

The key must be about dying to self—that those who lose their lives will find them. The rewards of this death may be to see God, for no one can see him and live. Perhaps that is what the verse means when it says, 'A good measure, pressed down, shaken together and running over will be put in your lap.'

Primary school teacher Mary Deaves writes:

After starting my first full-time teaching job in September 1997, I was looking forward to Christmas. It had been an enjoyable but busy term, with a class of 30 infants. I needed a rest, but Mum was preparing everything in our family and my mind turned to filling up my holiday. Before starting my job, I'd popped down a few times to our local night shelter, which is always busy because it is one of the few places for miles around where a homeless person can find a bed for the night. I knew they needed volunteers for Sundays and Bank Holidays and I knew that was what I had to do! I looked up the number in the phone book and, as I spoke to the warden, was amazed to learn that just that day, desperate for help, she had been trying to find my number to ring me!

I started helping there the next day and continued the whole Christmas season, befriending the residents and listening to them. On Christmas Day, we managed to get rid of four huge spare turkeys and we had to stay open during New Year's Day as lots of people needed a bed, to nurse their sore heads. God enabled me to be generous, and refreshed me so I could continue to keep on giving. I found it a privilege to see what it was like to be homeless, as Jesus was at his birth.

Since then, I've helped at the night shelter at least once a month and I know I gain more than I could ever give. I've found out about different life experiences and life views. I've learnt how to interact with different people— the kind of people Jesus spent time with. God has changed my heart towards the poor and marginalized in society. I didn't have much to give, except time, but I proved the truth of 2 Corinthians 9:11: 'He will always make you rich enough to be generous at all times' (GNB). And my involvement really does all stem from that Advent calling.*

For those of us who are hard-hearted, God, please soften us and teach us your ways.

---

* Since writing this, Mary has moved to a tough inner-city estate where she uses her home to reach out to young people, as well as teaching infants full-time.

4 January

Take delight in the Lord, and he will give you the desires of
your heart. Commit your way to the Lord; trust in him, and he
will act. He will make your vindication shine like the light,
and the justice of your cause like the noonday. Be still before
the Lord, and wait patiently for him; do not fret over those
who prosper in their way.

PSALM 37:4–7

At theme parks, where waits of over an hour for a two-minute ride are
not uncommon, management sends along people dressed as cartoon
characters to 'entertain' the queue. How much more, if we've got to
'wait patiently' for something, does it make sense to spend the time
'taking delight in the Lord'? But I'm usually far too busy fretting,
worrying and running in small circles, fruitlessly trying to make things
happen. I can look back with a smile now at myself, aged 20, walking
along the road, chanting these verses like a mantra. All my college
friends were getting engaged and I wanted, how I wanted, to be
married! I feared that, having reached this advanced age I would
obviously remain single for the rest of my life, destined to die on the
mission-field of some flyblown country. All of this was ruining my
sleep, my enjoyment of life and my relationship with God. It took a
long time before I acknowledged the truth of those words for me, but
I learnt a lot about seeking God in the process.

The spirit of our age is 'instant everything', from cappuccino to
credit cards to e-mail. The thought of waiting, even for such an
august being as the Lord, well, it's almost against our religion!
Anyway, he has the oddest idea of time. He always leaves everything
until the last minute, or later, and then sends so many answers to
your prayers at once that you're overwhelmed and experience a

whole new set of problems—usually concerning time management!

Students Paul Kingsley-Smith and Katherine Lyons have both worked in big supermarkets during the Christmas vacation. I asked them what it was like:

Incredibly busy, especially the week or two before Christmas when all the customers want the same thing and you're running around stacking shelves and everyone's stressed and you never want to see another turkey! There's always someone who's not impressed—the manager, the customers. Because checkout queues are long, when customers eventually reach the front they're often cross. It's a good time to try to be nice—to live out our faith. The 'stressier' people become, the nicer you try to be.

Then, on the 24th, you're frantically trying to sell off the fresh food for about 10p and after two days of calm you're back restocking empty shelves again. The shop's not so busy but lots of people arrive in a panic because they forgot that life continues after Christmas Day. Others are stocking up for New Year's parties. Working there was quite an experience—but one we enjoyed, on the whole!

Teach us to be still for a few moments today, Lord, and simply to enjoy the rest and refreshment you give us, whether we have too much to do or too little.

5 January

On entering the house, they saw the child with Mary his mother; and they knelt down and paid him homage. Then, opening their treasure chests, they offered him gifts of gold, frankincense, and myrrh.

MATTHEW 2:11

Often the Bible surprises us, posing more questions than it gives answers. Here we have not Jews or Christians, but astrologers who come from the mystic East to present rich, strange gifts as homage to the infant Jesus. Did their chests contain other treasures from which they chose three, or did they give everything? Was it by divination or research that they knew those particular spices formed part of the recipe for the Jews' holy anointing oil, or that the most significant objects within the Holy of Holies contained gold? Could it have been that these occult practitioners were alone among humankind at the time in being aware that this infant was High Priest, King and God?

What became of the gifts? Presumably they were accepted, though many of us would not deign to receive gifts from astrologers or magi (shamans). Did they finance the flight into Egypt? If not, what use were the perfumes with their brief half-life? To relieve the stress and anxiety of the moment, as aromatherapy asserts? Or, as the sense of smell acted on the subconscious, were they a reminder of death, of bodies spice-bound for burial—foreshadowing events to come?

What drove the astrologers to follow the star all that way in the first place? For what reason were they overwhelmed with joy when it stopped? Because it signified the end of a terrible journey, the beginning of a wonder, or both? What became of the astrologers after they took the long, unfamiliar road back to their own country? Will we meet them in heaven?

We know only that they were givers and pilgrims, that it cost and inconvenienced them, that they didn't understand everything (the danger from Herod, for example). We know that these powerful and wealthy foreigners paid homage to an ordinary-looking baby who really did turn out to be the Son of God. By this they are judged and for this reason we are reading their story 2,000 years later. They came and they gave.

Father-of-two Paul Cox is on the core leadership team of his church, looks after its finances and its 18–30s group, but also works full-time, commuting to London where he has a senior position with BT.

Phew! I've made it. It's nearly the end of the first week back at work after the holiday break. If I didn't know better, I would say that everyone had saved their most pressing issues for me to resolve in their absence (on holiday). It's certainly been a challenging week and it has taken its toll. On days like this I wonder just how much more I have to give. The expense of Christmas and New Year celebrations soon becomes a stark reality when the credit card bill arrives—the almost constant round of hospitality given to friends and family, the contribution made to local church life, and so it goes on.

And yet I will keep on giving—of myself, my time, money, love, friendship, possessions, of all that I am and have. It's the way I am, it's what I want to do; not naturally but supernaturally. Because that's what God has made me. His total sacrifice for me requires a response—a life of giving, following his example.

This year, what is God asking us to give, as individuals, as families, as churches? To whom is he asking us to present our gifts, of money, time, talents, ourselves? As we re-examine his priorities for us, let's ask him also how to give—and especially that we might draw on him so that, in giving, we might always find more to give.

6 January

'Blessed are those who hunger and thirst for righteousness, for they will be filled.'

MATTHEW 5:6

So, what does hungering after righteousness mean? Not to hunger after getting and grabbing, but to give; not to be liked, but to love; not to strive for our rights and revenge, but to forgive. Not thirsting to feed our pride and achieve recognition, but for humility; not pushing for what we want to fulfil ourselves, but thirsting for what God wants—and to serve others.

The Bible doesn't say that we'll be filled with righteousness by wallowing in guilt over our sin and shortcomings, but by 'thirsting' for it, starving for it, longing with all our beings to be holy as God is holy, longing to follow his ways, to be near him, to be filled.

The special time of Christmas is over now; the new year is establishing its own routine and this book is at an end. But Emmanuel, God's gift to us at Christmas, is still with us, alongside the Holy Spirit, our Comforter, our Advocate, who gives us power to live aright.

Rosemary Conley, diet and fitness expert, writes:

At the beginning of a new year, after all the over-indulgences of the festive season, many people resolve to go on a diet and to do more exercise. I say, get into some good habits with God, too! Give him a higher prominence in your life by more regular Bible study. Make your prayer time at the beginning of the day, rather than while you are doing something else. When we ask God for help, we expect his undivided attention—shouldn't we give him ours?

Dear Lord, we do want to give you our undivided attention, not just at special seasons but throughout the year.

When we're exhausted, may we turn to you in expectation and be lifted up on your wings.

When we're disappointed, may your joy delight our hearts like a kingfisher on a dull day.

When we're in the midst of conflict or feel lonely or rejected, may we be fuelled by your amazing love to keep on loving others.

When pain or anxiety rob us of your peace, be our Prince, hold us close and never let us go.

When we're racing around trying to uphold all kinds of traditions, may we stop—and risk leaning on you instead.

And when we're caught up in establishing our security and comfort in this world, may your generosity overwhelm us, that we might give and give and keep on giving, just as you do.

Thank you that you came and lived among us on this earth at Christmas time so many years ago. May we learn your heart and your ways, that a little more of your kingdom might come on this earth, as it is established in heaven.

DAY BY DAY WITH GOD

You may be interested to know that Chris Leonard is a regular contributor to *Day by Day with God*, the regular Bible reading notes published jointly by BRF and Christina Press. *Day by Day with God* provides daily notes, including a short printed Bible passage, which explains and applies God's word, written by women who have themselves found the Bible an invaluable guide and encouragement. Whether life for you is over-busy or seems empty, you will be inspired and encouraged as you try to make sense of life and God's purposes for you each day.

The following is an extract from readings by Chris Leonard which appear in the September–December 2001 issue of *Day by Day with God*.

Matters of the heart

Love the Lord your God with all your heart and with all your soul and with all your mind.

When we read anything, including the Bible, most of us use mainly our minds—we're taught that way in school. But we're going to focus now on matters of the heart—and I don't mean either triple bypass operations or the Valentine 'lurv' of the magazines and soaps.

When a fledgling blackbird flew at top speed into the glass of our patio doors a moment ago, my heart beat faster and my stomach lurched. I tiptoed forward, willing it still to be uninjured, somehow. The sight of its stiff little body made me wince for its hardworking parents. They even fought off magpies that attacked their nest!

Our bodies react in physical ways to emotions as well as to danger— guts churn and hearts beat faster. Down-to-earth Hebrews often referred to 'guts' in Old Testament passages which modern Christians have translated as 'heart'. The Hebrew word for compassion doesn't pull any punches. It means 'a churning of the bowels'!

Heart (or gut) reactions matter and the Bible has a huge wealth of things to say about them. Our hearts/guts are described variously as hard, proud, perverse or calloused; as contrite, responsive, happy or secure; as anxious, humble, broken or faint; and as pure, faithful, upright and even 'circumcised'! Why are they so important? Because they govern our relationships with God and with one another. Jesus said, 'Out of the overflow of the heart the mouth speaks. The good man brings good things out of the good stored up in him, and the evil man brings evil things out of the evil stored up in him' (Matthew 12:34–35).

Lord, help me to understand, and to feel, more of the heart of the matter —of your heart, of my heart, of my neighbour's heart. Help me to understand, and work out in practice, how all of these can meet, and beat, together.

God's heart

How can I give you up, Ephraim? How can I hand you over, Israel?
... My heart is changed within me; all my compassion is aroused.
I will not carry out my fierce anger, nor will I turn and devastate
Ephraim. For I am God, and not man—the Holy One among you.
I will not come in wrath.

Listen to some sermons and you'd think that Christianity's main concern was sorting out complicated details of theology and background—so that we can believe six impossible things about God, if not before, then after, breakfast.

But we're not following some system of philosophy. We may try to understand God with our minds but in the end it will prove impossible. He's so much bigger than we are! He gave us brains to use, but we'll only truly begin to get to know him as we worship and walk with him. That's the totally amazing part! Christians are people who, through no merit of their own, form a relationship with God and begin to discover more about his heart.

And what a heart! Never remote or impassive, throughout the Old Testament God demonstrates heart-feelings of anger, exuberance, love and compassion far stronger than ours. Yet as various human beings whom he trusts speak and interact with him, he'll change heart, sparing a city, forgiving an individual, extending a life.

In today's passage, yet again God's chosen people Israel had refused to turn back to him. By rights, God said, he should destroy them utterly, yet, 'It was I who taught Ephraim to walk, taking them by the arms; but they did not realize it was I who healed them... I lifted the yoke from their neck and bent down to feed them' (Hosea 11:3–4). How can anyone with such a tender father's heart give up his children? God asks himself. We feel his agony. And we catch a glimpse of what is at the heart of his being.

May I not grieve your heart, Lord, but make it glad!

Jesus' heart

Now my heart is troubled, and what shall I say?
'Father, save me from this hour'? No, it was for this very reason
I came to this hour.

Jesus had the biggest heart, reaching out to all kinds of people—family, friends and enemies; strangers, children and women. He revelled in parties but also needed time alone with his Father to share emotions ranging from anger to sadness, joy to compassion. But of himself, the amazingly great Son of Almighty God said, 'Take my yoke upon you and learn from me, *for I am gentle and humble in heart*, and you will find rest for your souls' (Matthew 11:29, my italics).

Most Christians relate more easily to Jesus than to the Father. I've always found it the other way round, but recently have been looking closer at this extraordinary God-man. Was it because Jesus responded so exactly to God's heartbeat that he did such surprising things on earth, rarely choosing the way people expected him to go? Some of the things he said and did, I still don't understand, but I do know that, as 'God with us', Jesus came to live among ordinary people, sharing their joys and despair, loving both them and his Father with all of his heart. Being a 'bridge too far' between sinful man and a holy God brought him in the end to Gethsemane. His heart troubled way beyond the stomach-churning stage, he sweated agonizing drops of blood there. Finally he gave his heart, quite literally. From it, water and life-blood flowed as the Roman soldier's spear pierced his side shortly after he died on the cross. Even today, that water and blood wash us clean, making us fit to stand before the Father and share his life.

Jesus endured all that, Hebrews says, for the joy that was set before him. What joy? Surely not being in heaven with his Father, or he wouldn't have come to earth at all. No, his death brought him the joy of knowing us better.

What heart-love! Thank you, Jesus!

Hearts unlike God's—divided

*So Solomon did evil in the eyes of the Lord; he did not follow the
Lord completely, as David his father had done.*

One way our hearts often differ from God's is that ours are divided.
We'll 'buy' the gospel as we buy 'pick and mix' sweets, taking only the
selection that we like.

David's son Solomon had everything going for him—wisdom, riches,
God's promises. He even met directly with God, twice. Yet he let his
weakness for women (1000 of them, which seems excessive, to say the
least!) seduce him into following their gods. God took objection to his
heart-attitude, which had strayed a long way from the humility, gratitude and desire for righteousness that had been so outstanding in his
father. God told Solomon, 'Since this is your attitude and you have not
kept my covenant… which I commanded you, I will most certainly tear
the kingdom away from you' (v. 11).

What's my weakness? What, like a wedge, has the potential, little
by little, to divide my heart from God's? Do I buy into materialism
for the security or the kudos? Do I put 'religious' observance before
unselfish love? There's a sweatshirt slogan which reads, 'I'd rather be
fishing!' Whatever it is that God has asked me to do, am I begrudging
about it because there is always something else which I'd rather be
doing—and does that 'something' take priority at times when I know
it shouldn't? Does fear, or longing, cause me to put my faith (only half-
seriously of course) in horoscopes or similar things? Do I trust lotteries
or pension and insurance schemes more than God? Or do I trust and
worship him with an undivided heart, at least for most of the time,
returning wholeheartedly when I've strayed, as David did? Is my love
for God as unconditional as his for me?

---

*Teach me your way, O Lord, and I will walk in your truth; give me an
undivided heart, that I may fear your name (Psalm 86:11).*

Hearts unlike God's—stubborn, deceitful

He looked round at them in anger and, deeply distressed at their stubborn hearts, said to the man, 'Stretch out your hand.'

Late one hot Sunday afternoon, when we lived in a terraced house, a horrible thing happened. Our neighbour's oldest child, a loving and sensitive girl of about ten, had brought her class's rabbit home for the weekend. The whole family had been making a fuss of it, much to their dog's annoyance. When someone left the back door open, the inevitable happened. Dog pounced on rabbit—and rabbit was dead within seconds.

The whole family was distraught. It would have been bad enough had the pet been their own, but a whole classful of children loved this one! The mother, who had long resisted weekend rabbit entertaining on the grounds that this might happen, blamed herself for giving in. All three children, wailing loudly, accused each other of leaving the door open. The dog howled—why did no one love him any more? Unfortunately, though, we couldn't stay to comfort our neighbours as we were off to church. Next day we learnt that Sue, who lived two doors the other side of us, had been there for them all evening. Sue had only just become a Christian but, as she said, 'No point going to church to hear about loving people when you have an opportunity to actually do it!'

Ouch—my heart can be as stubborn and uncaring as a Pharisee's! When God's Son came among them, healing the sick, they quibbled about ways in which he might have broken the Sabbath law—which was there to help people anyway. Jesus must have felt as Jeremiah prophesied, 'The heart is deceitful above all things and beyond cure; who can understand it?'

Lord, sometimes my heart is apathetic. When I don't care enough, I've even used you as an excuse. I can be cynical and perverse, deceitful and stubborn—so unlike you. Sometimes I do feel 'beyond cure'. Give me a new heart, one more like yours!

Hearts unlike God's—hard

*Today if you hear his voice, do not harden your hearts as you did...
that day at Massah in the desert where your fathers tried and tested
me, though they had seen what I did.*

What if Jackie Pullinger hadn't obeyed God's voice to get off a ship
where he told her—in Hong Kong? What if John Wesley hadn't listened
when God told him the world was his parish—if he'd stayed put instead
of riding thousands of miles on horseback, preaching the gospel to
ordinary people? What if Lord Shaftesbury hadn't listened when God
told him to keep up the fight to improve conditions for the mentally ill
and for children down mines; or Nelson Mandela hadn't listened to
what God was telling him about forgiveness? If they'd all hardened their
hearts and opted for a quiet life, maybe others would have stepped in,
but meanwhile, how much extra suffering would the world have seen?

Each of those obedient people had first experienced the supreme
heart-softener of God's grace. The hearts of those who resist grace can
grow so hard that they become impervious to God. As Jesus said in
Matthew 13:15, 'For this people's heart has become calloused; they
hardly hear with their ears, and they have closed their eyes.' I'm writing
this on holiday in Austria, where the tour guide told us that the prince-
archbishops who used to rule over the rich Salzkammergut area
expelled all the Protestants who lived there. A month ago I stayed in
a house with a priest hole, where Catholic priests, fearing for their
lives, once hid from Protestants. Often the *church* persecuted gospel
preachers and those who translated the Bible into languages which
ordinary people could read. It doesn't make Christianity sound like
wonderful news, does it?

---

*Help me never to become so proud and hard-hearted that I'm shut off
from your grace, Lord. For I need to turn and repent, to find healing and
rediscover your way ahead so many times each day.*

Heart surgery

One of those listening was a woman named Lydia… a worshipper of God. The Lord opened her heart to respond to Paul's message.

Not the misogynist that people think he was, Paul was speaking specifically to women here—women who had gathered to pray outside the city gates of Philippi. Lydia, a rich businesswoman, worshipped God. But if she *had* heard about Jesus before, the message hadn't struck home until God 'opened her heart' that day. I'm sure we've all known times when God has opened our heart in a similar way, causing us to respond to some new aspect of himself.

In a more dramatic example, after being knocked around by husbands and lovers, 'Sal' was abandoned with various children. My friend 'Lin' had become her friend. For ten years she told Sal about Jesus. Sal came to believe, but drew back from the implications of committing herself. Finally she agreed to attend an Alpha course. In the final few hours of the course weekend away, she allowed Lin and me to pray for her. But then, 'You'll have to stop!' she gasped. 'I'm having a dizzy spell or something.'

'That's the Holy Spirit,' explained Lin.

'Really?' Suddenly her troubled look was replaced by a huge smile. She'd met God! As he did with Lydia (an altogether different type of woman), the Lord opened Sal's heart in that moment and afterwards there was no stopping her. She told everyone she knew, she joined the church, got baptized and slowly, with the help of God and Christian friends, she began to work through some of the huge problems in her life.

Thank you, Father, that whether we're respectable, religious people or not, you're willing to send Christ to dwell in our hearts. Then you put your Spirit in our hearts as a deposit as well, guaranteeing what is to come. You're surely the greatest heart surgeon of all, since you take away our hearts of stone and give us hearts of flesh.

Circumcised hearts!

You stiff-necked people, with uncircumcised hearts and ears! You are just like your fathers: You always resist the Holy Spirit.

A neighbour had recently given birth by Caesarean section, so she couldn't drive. As I took her to collect a prescription, she explained that their Rabbi had circumcised the tiny baby two days before and that their GP thought his worsening infection stemmed from the home-operation. We both winced as she described the process. As it turned out, the illness had nothing to do with her baby's circumcision, but I still thank God that he's dropped that particular requirement for Christians!

We don't escape entirely though. Circumcision never was about a purely physical operation. Romans 2:29 talks about 'circumcision of the heart, by the Spirit, not by the written code'. Whatever does that mean? In scripture, sometimes an uncircumcised heart and a stiff neck are paralleled. I know that a stiff neck makes me inflexible—for example, when I'm driving, looking both ways at road junctions becomes difficult. The words from today's reading are spoken by Stephen, the first Christian to be stoned to death for his faith. The Jews who threw the stones wouldn't allow their hearts to be opened to the gospel truth he proclaimed. In effect, they thought they knew the law better than God. Proud and inflexible, their actions became terrible. As for circumcision of the ears(!), look again at Jesus' words in Matthew 13:15, from Saturday's reading.

Jewish males are marked physically by circumcision as a sign of their faith, of their Jewishness. In theory they're marked as ones who will obey God's law, but God had always wanted their hearts to be marked too, like David's. Today he practises special non-invasive heart surgery on the hearts of Christian men *and* women, if we co-operate. But what kind of a new, improved, marked heart is he after? We'll have a brief look at some of the qualities in the next few days.

In the meanwhile consider the kind of heart-qualities you'd want in a husband or lifelong friend.

Happy hearts

A happy heart makes the face cheerful,
but heartache crushes the spirit.

If you've been thinking about what heart-qualities you might look for in a lasting friendship, you might find it interesting to glance at one of those lonely hearts pages found in freebie local papers. Many people specify not only age, looks, background, interests and so on, but something called 'GSOH'. This intrigued me. Having cynically assumed that the letter 'S' stood for a three-letter word ending in 'x', I had real problems trying to work out the rest. In fact, the initials stand for 'good sense of humour'—which, as any right-minded person knows, is far more important than sex in a lasting relationship!

It's not just hilarity—wouldn't we all choose to spend time with people who believe the glass is half-full, rather than half-empty, with people who look cheerful rather than miserable? I have a friend who sees good in everything. Occasionally this makes me want to hit her, but most of the time I love to be with her. Even her e-mails lift my heart. Though not a Christian, she makes every effort to seek out and appreciate beauty and goodness in little things and to encourage everyone. Since her sister died young, she's felt it is her mission in life to spread happiness around her. I think God likes that!

However, some people have experienced such heartache that their spirits end up crushed, and that's a terrible thing. Jesus promised to be there for such people, not to despise or break them but to nurture and mend over time.

Lord Jesus, you were anointed with the oil of joy above your companions and crowds wanted to be with you. Give us something of your happy heart and cheerful face—make us attractive for you. And for those whose hearts ache and whose spirits are crushed right now, you've known that too. Will you bring into their lives people who will share a little bit of happiness with them, as much as they can bear at the present time?

Pure hearts

*Create in me a pure heart, O God, and renew a
steadfast spirit within me.*

David wrote this psalm after the prophet Nathan had confronted him
over his sin with Bathsheba. Few of us will have done anything as
wicked as causing the death of our lover's spouse, but there again, if
asked, few would feel that our hearts were pure or our spirits steadfast.
We'd all acknowledge, it's vital to any relationship that each partner
remains true and trustworthy—that they don't betray each other.
Certainly God sees it that way. He's really tough about it. Jesus said it is
the pure in heart who will see God! (Matthew 5:8).

But the word translated 'pure' here means 'clean'. Dirty, impure
things can be made clean! From the same word comes 'catharsis', which
has the sense of being purged, as when emotions are brought to the
surface and released through watching a tragic drama. We can 'take
heart' from David who, despite knowing none of the benefits bought for
us by the drama of Jesus' death on the cross, asked that God would
'create' a pure heart and 'renew' a steadfast spirit within him.

We all waver; we're not always pure or steadfast; but we do have
times when our hearts are right with God, when we love him and long
to serve him with all of our being. He notices when we serve him
faithfully through the petty irritations and setbacks of everyday life.
And when we become impure, when we run off doing our own thing,
afterwards God can clean our hearts, recreating and renewing the bits
we've spoilt.

David didn't stay wallowing in the grief of his repentance for ever.
After turning from his sin, he set his face firmly in God's direction and,
with God's help, moved forward. May we do the same after
transgressions great or small.

---

*Is there any area of your heart which you're not allowing God to renew,
because you're too ashamed of it?*

Responsive hearts

But Hezekiah's heart was proud and he did not respond to the kindness shown him; therefore the Lord's wrath was on him and on Judah and Jerusalem.

Hezekiah must have been fantastic at praying. There he was, king of little Judah, with his capital city, Jerusalem, under siege to the ridiculously strong armies of the superpower of the day—Assyria. Then Hezekiah prayed and God's angel slaughtered all the enemy troops overnight. The mighty Assyrian king, Sennacherib, had to limp back home in disgrace. It's comparable to all the US armed forces being annihilated under mysterious circumstances while attacking Andorra!

Shortly after this astounding victory, King Hezekiah fell ill, seriously ill. About to die, he prayed, and again God heard and gave him a miraculous sign. 'Wow,' thought Hezekiah, 'I've done it again—my prayers are really something!' Spiritual success gives a heady feeling of power but also heralds a dangerous time. Maybe our church prays, someone's miraculously healed of cancer and we're all over the moon—got healing sorted now! It's easy to take our eyes off God and assume that we ourselves are the answer to all kinds of problems.

We can respond to God's kindness rightly, with gratitude and humility, or we can respond wrongly, in pride. In the end Hezekiah proved to have the right kind of responsive heart. He repented in time to prevent God's anger turning on him and his people. God healed him and he continued to reign as one of the best kings to grace the pages of the Old Testament. Hezekiah faced testing times—a massive enemy attack and serious illness. Yet after a serious setback caused by his mistaken heart-attitude, his responsive, praying heart released God's goodness again.

Blessed are those whose strength is in you, who have set their hearts on pilgrimage. As they pass through the valley of Baca [weeping], they make it a place of springs (Psalm 84:5–6).

God, we don't want to have proud hearts, but responsive hearts, pilgrim hearts, hearts touched by you.

Take heart!

*I have told you these things, so that in me you may have peace.
In this world you will have trouble. But take heart!
I have overcome the world.*

One small word causes Christians a lot of trouble—the word 'should'. After reading these Bible notes, it will be all too easy to think, 'Oh dear, I *should* have a pure, godly heart, steadfast, responsive and without pride. I *should* be happy, and today's verse implies that I *should* be peaceful too, even though it promises me lots of trouble as well! I don't stand a chance!'

But that doesn't take into account Jesus' heart for us. His words in the verse above aren't some kind of cruel parody of the song: 'Though there's trouble ahead, you'd better face the music and dance... or else!' No, he tells us to 'take heart'. Why? Because he has (not 'we should') overcome the world, with all its sin and sorrow. In the end we're secure not in the rightness of our own hearts, but because he holds us close to his heart.

Isaiah 40:11 reminds us, 'He tends his flock like a shepherd: he gathers the lambs in his arms and carries them close to his heart; he gently leads those that have young.' Sheep can race about in wild-eyed panic, doing themselves all kinds of damage. They have peace only because they follow the shepherd who looks after them, shields them from danger, overcomes their enemies and leads them to food, water and shelter. If their hearts follow the good shepherd, who knows their silly ways but still cares enough to give his life for them, they can't go very far wrong

---

May we forget about the 'shoulds'. May we nestle close to your heart, where everything begins to make sense. As we begin to appreciate the love that's in your heart, may ours melt and change, becoming more like yours. May we, whatever our circumstances, take heart in all that you are, in all that you have done and will do. Amen